Pocket (... Script

Dr. Fayeq Oweis

Hippocrene Books, Inc.

New York, NY

For information, address:
HIPPOCRENE BOOKS, INC.
171 Madison Ave.
New York, NY 10016
www.hippocrenebooks.com

  Library of Congress Cataloging-in-Publication Data

Oweis, Fayeq.
  Pocket guide to Arabic script : [al-lughah al-'Arabåiyah]
  Fayeq Oweis.
      p. cm.
  Subtitle in Arabic script.
  ISBN-13: 978-0-7818-1104-0
  ISBN-10: 0-7818-1104-X
  1. Arabic language--Writing. I. Title: Lughah al-'Arabåiyah.
  II. Title.
  PJ6123.O94 2005
  492.71'1--dc22

                                                    2005052776

Printed in the United States of America.

Table of Contents
المحتويات

Table of Contents

المحتويات

This book would not have been possible without the help and support of many colleagues and students. Many thanks to the Department of Foreign Languages and Literatures at San Francisco State University and to my Arabic language students for their support, feedback, and input during the preparation of this work.

Fayeq Oweis, Ph.D.
San Francisco State University

Organization of the Guide

The Arabic alphabet. Covered letters are in white on black.

The letters's name and shape, with transliteration, pronunciation, and notes

The shape of the letter based on its location in a word, with examples for each variation.

The letter in different positions.

Handwriting instructions with the direction and order of strokes.

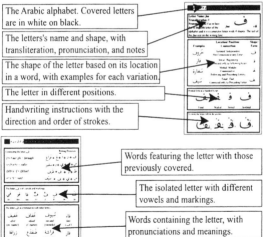

Words featuring the letter with those previously covered.

The isolated letter with different vowels and markings.

Words containing the letter, with pronunciations and meanings.

The letter in different calligraphic styles.

1

The Arabic Language:

Arabic belongs to the Semitic languages, a group within the Afroasiatic family. (The Modern Semitic languages are Arabic, Hebrew, Aramaic/Assyrian, and Amharic/Ethiopian.) Prevalent throughout the Middle East and North Africa, Arabic is the official language of 22 Arab nations and spoken by over 220 million people. Because of its status as the liturgical language of Islam, it is also used in the faith's practice by over one billion Muslims worldwide. It is spoken by more than 4 million people in the U.S. and has been adopted by the United Nations as one of its six official languages.

The Arabic language can be divided into three categories:

  1- Classical of Historical Arabic (e.g. the *Qur'an* and pre-Islamic poetry).
  2- Literary or Modern Standard Arabic (MSA), also called *fus-Haa*. This
     is the contemporary Arabic used in publishing and other media. It is the
     language as it is taught in schools worldwide, including the Middle East.
  3- Spoken Arabic, also called *ᶜamiyya*, which is the informal Arabic heard
     in everyday life. This category contains all regional dialects, including
     Egyptian, Moroccan, and Levantine or Eastern Arabic.

The Arabic Script:

The oldest extant example of written Arabic appears on a Syrian tombstone dated 328 A.D. The *Qur'an*, the sacred book of Islam, dates to the 7th century. It is the language's first written document, providing the model for Arabic syntax and grammar. Originally written on parchment, scapula, and the leaf stalks of date palms, its various sections were collected into one manuscript after the death of Prophet Muhammad in 632 A.D. Copies were transcribed during the reign of Caliph Uthman shortly thereafter. The four or five produced were sent to different regions and used as sources for additional copies. These early versions of the *Qur'an* were written in a slanted, non-vocalized, and non-dotted script. In the 8th century, dots, non-letter alphabetic symbols, and other vocalization features were added to ensure that Islam's newly faithful could read and recite from the *Qur'an* correctly.

Basic Facts about the Arabic Language:

Arabic is not a difficult language to learn and understand. The chart on page 4 shows the entire alphabet with corresponding English sound. It also shows the shape of each letter depending on its location in a word. The chart of page 5 indicates the symbols and short vowels that are used in vocalized text. Refer to these charts only after becoming familiar with the entire guide.

Here are some key features of Arabic:

▸ The alphabet contains 28 letters, three functioning as long vowels and consonants.

▸ Arabic is written from right to left.

▸ Letters do not have capital or lowercase forms.

▸ There is no distinction between print and cursive. All letters in a word are joined.

▸ Most letters change form or shape according to their location in the word (initial, medial, final, or isolated).

▸ Arabic script has two layers: the core of the letters and the alphabetical markings (i.e. short vowels).

▸ Arabic pronunciation has a one-to-one correspondence between sounds and written letters.

▸ Arabic words are generally written as they are pronounced.

Pronunciations:

Most Arabic letters have sounds equivalent to those in English. Few letters are unique to the Arabic language, and these have been noted in this guide. A number of Arabic letters have *emphatic* counterparts (called velarized consonants), which are more saturated (deeper) and produced in the back of the throat. The emphatic letters have been transliterated with capitals. They affect the quality of the surrounding letters and vowels by giving them a deeper quality.

This guide is intended for general English speaking audience with no or little knowledge of Arabic. It is a comprehensive reference to Arabic script and the writing system, serving the needs of those who aim to read and write Arabic. It also serves as a companion to other books that teach the Arabic language or its grammar.

The Arabic Alphabet and the shapes of the letters

Letter Name	Transliteration	Pronunciation & English Equivalent	Final (End)	Middle Position	Initial Beginning	Isolated Alone	اسم الحرف
*alif	'a , 'u, 'i		ا	ا	ا	ا	الف
baa	b	b as in bake	ب	ـبـ	بـ	ب	باء
taa	t	t as in take	ـت	ـتـ	تـ	ت	تاء
thaa	th	th as in thin	ـث	ـثـ	ثـ	ث	ثاء
jiim	j	j as in joke	ـج	ـجـ	جـ	ج	جيم
Haa	H (h)**	no equivalent	ـح	ـحـ	حـ	ح	حاء
khaa	kh	no equivalent	ـخ	ـخـ	خـ	خ	خاء
daal	d	d as in day	ـد	ـد	د	د	دال
dhaal	dh	th as in this	ـذ	ـذ	ذ	ذ	ذال
raa	r	r as in car	ـر	ـر	ر	ر	راء
zaay	z	z as in zeal	ـز	ـز	ز	ز	زاي
siin	s	s as in snake	ـس	ـسـ	سـ	س	سين
shiin	sh	sh as in shake	ـش	ـشـ	شـ	ش	شين
Saad	S (ş)	emphatic s	ـص	ـصـ	صـ	ص	صاد
Daad	D (ḍ)	emphatic d	ـض	ـضـ	ضـ	ض	ضاد
Taa	T (ṭ)	emphatic t	ـط	ـطـ	ط	ط	طاء
DHaa	DH (z)	emphatic dh	ـظ	ـظـ	ظ	ظ	ظاء
'ayn	' (')	no equivalent	ـع	ـعـ	عـ	ع	عين
ghayn	gh	no equivalent	ـغ	ـغـ	غـ	غ	غين
faa	f	as in face	ـف	ـفـ	فـ	ف	فاء
qaaf	q	emphatic k	ـق	ـقـ	قـ	ق	قاف
kaaf	k	as in key	ـك	ـكـ	كـ	ك	كاف
laam	l	as in leaf	ـل	ـلـ	لـ	ل	لام
miim	m	as in make	ـم	ـمـ	مـ	م	ميم
nuun	n	as in none	ـن	ـنـ	نـ	ن	نون
haa	h	as in hat	ـه	ـهـ	هـ	ه	هاء
*waaw	w	as in wake	ـو	ـو	و	و	واو
*yaa	y	as in yell	ـي	ـيـ	يـ	ي	ياء

*alif (ا), waaw (و), and yaa (ي) also function as long vowels. (ا) as "aa" (ā), (و) as "uu" (ū), (ي) as "ii" (ī)
** The transliteration letters in brackets with dots below them are based on the Library of Congress transliteration system.

4

Short Vowels / Pronunciation Markers / Alphabetical Symbols

The Arabic language has a number of alphabetical and pronunciation symbols. Some of these symbols, such as short vowels, are optional additions in standard text and may be omitted. Other symbols are part of the Arabic script and cannot be omitted. The chart below shows the name, shape, and usage of these symbols.

Name/ Notes/ Usage	Shape	Name in Arabic
fat-Ha - Short vowel "a" placed over consonants	َ	فتحة
Damma - Short vowel "u" placed over consonants	ُ	ضمة
kasra - Short vowel "i" placed under consonants	ِ	كسرة
sukuun - Absence of a vowel, placed over consonants	ْ	سكون
hamza - Glottal Stop. It may appear as follows: ء أ إ ئ ؤ لأ لإ	ء	همزة
shadda - Doubling of a consonant; placed over it	ّ	شدة
taa marbuuTa - Indicates a feminine gender (only occurs at the end of a word)	ة ﺔ	تاء مربوطة
waSla - Elidable or connecting *hamza*	ٱ	وصلة
alif madda - Lengthening the *alif*; replaces ١+أ	آ	الف مدة
Dagger *alif* - Pronounced like regular *alif*	ٰ	الف مخفية
alif in the shape of a *yaa* (only at the end of a word)	ى	الف مقصورة
tanwiin al-fatH - Grammatical ending, pronounced "an"	ً	تنوين الفتح
tanwiin aD-Damm - Grammatical ending, pronounced "un"	ٌ	تنوين الضم
tanwiin al-kasr - Grammatical ending, pronounced "in"	ٍ	تنوين الكسر
laam- alif - Combination of the letters ل and ١	لا	لام الف
alif-laam - The definite article	ال	الف لام

5

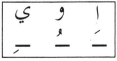

Arabic has three long vowels and three short ones. The long vowels are represented by letters of the alphabet, while the short vowels are symbols placed over or below consonants. The letters *alif*, *waaw* and *yaa* function as long vowels, which are twice as long as short vowels. The short vowel symbols are called *fat-Ha (a)*, *Damma (u)* and *kasra (i)*. Two other symbols are also found in Arabic: one, called *sukuun*, that represents an absence of a vowel, and one, called *shadda*, that represents the doubling of the consonant. The following examples show both long and short vowels with the letter *taa* (ت). In standard text, such as newspapers and books, vowels and alphabetical symbols are omitted. One has to deduce the short vowels, so, the more vocabulary is mastered, the easier it is to read non-vocalized text.

Long Vowels		
the letter *yaa* as a long vowel	**the letter *waaw* as a long vowel**	**the letter *alif* as a long vowel**
ياء	واو	الف
ي	و	ا
pronounced (*ii*)	pronounced (*uu*)	pronounced (*aa*)
تي = ي + ت	تو = و + ت	تا = ا + ت
t+ii=tii	*t+uu=tuu*	*t+aa=taa*
the letter *t* with *yaa* as a long vowel *ii*	the letter *t* with *waaw* as a long vowel *uu*	the letter *t* with *alif* as a long vowel *aa*

6

Arabic Vowels *al-Harakaat*   الحَرَكات

Short Vowels		
The short vowel *kasra*	**The short vowel** *Damma*	**The short vowel** *fat-Ha*
كَسرة	ضَمّة	فتحة
ِ	ُ	َ
Corresponds to English vowel (*i*) and placed below the letter	Corresponds to English vowel (*u*) and placed above the letter	Corresponds to English vowel (*a*) and placed above the letter
تِ	تُ	تَ
ti the letter *t* with a short vowel *i*	*tu* the letter *t* with a short vowel *u*	*ta* the letter *t* with a short vowel *a*

The **shadda** (شدّة) is a symbol for doubling the consonant and lengthening its pronunciation. It is represented with a shape similar to a miniature *w* placed over the consonant. ّ

tt (doubling the *t* as in the word *hotter*)   تّ

The **sukuun** (سُكون) is a symbol representing the absence of a vowel. It is a small circle placed over a consonant. ْ

The letter *kh* with no vowels as in *yakht* (yacht)   يَخْت

7

Letter Name: *alif*
Transliteration: aa (long vowel)
    'a, 'u, 'i (when serving
      as a *hamza* seat)

The *alif* is the first letter of the alphabet. It has two functions:
(1) It is a long vowel pronounced *aa* (twice as long as a short
vowel *a*) and it resembles the *a* sound in *bad*. It sometimes has
a deeper quality that resembles the *a* in *father*; (2) When the
alif comes at the beginning of a word, it serves as a seat for a
special sign called *hamza* (**ء**), which can carry three vowels:
'a, 'u, and **'i**. The *alif* is a non-connector letter with only two
shapes.

Examples	Location / Position / Connection	Shape / Form
اب	Isolated / Independent / Initial Not connected to any letter	ا
باب	Medial / Final / End Connected to preceding letter	...ـا

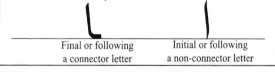

Printed form in standard script

    Final or following   Initial or following
    a connector letter   a non-connector letter

To write the letter, follow the arrows:

The *alif* (ا) and the *hamza* (ء):

Since words in Arabic cannot start with a vowel, the *alif* at the beginning of a word represents the *hamza* (ء) sign which is not part of the Arabic alphabet. The *hamza* can carry any of the short vowels (*fat-Ha a, Damma u, kasra i*), and its pronunciation is the same as these vowels. In this guide, an apostrophe (') followed by a short vowel indicates the presence of the *hamza*. Here are the variations of the letter (ا) representing the *hamza* (ء) at the beginning of a word and pronounced *a, u, i*:

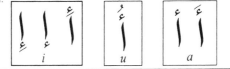

The letter ا as a long vowel **aa** and as a seat for the *hamza*:

أَخ
'akh (brother)
The *alif* as a seat for the *hamza* with a short vowel *a*

باب
baab (door)
The *alif* as a long vowel (aa)

إِبن
'ibn (son)
The *alif* as a seat for the *hamza* with a short vowel *i*

أُخت
'ukht (sister)
The *alif* as a seat for the *hamza* with a short vowel *u*

The letter ا in various calligraphic styles:

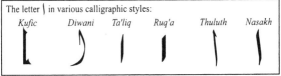

Kufic   Diwani   Ta'liq   Ruq'a   Thuluth   Nasakh

9

Letter Name: *baa*

Transliteration: b

Pronunciation: b as in bake

باء | *baa* | ب ب

The letter **baa** is the 2nd letter of the alphabet, and a connector letter with 4 shapes depending on its location (initial, medial, final, or not connected) in the word. The dot below the letter is an integral part of it.

Examples	Location / Position / Connection	Shape / Form
باب	Isolated / Independent Not connected to any letter	ب
با	Initial / Beginning Connected only to following letter	بـ...
ببا	Medial / Middle Connected to following and preceding letters	...ـبـ...
ببب	Final / End Connected only to preceding letter	ـب...

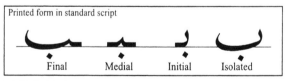

Printed form in standard script

Final   Medial   Initial   Isolated

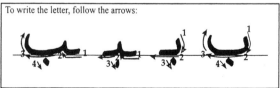

To write the letter, follow the arrows:

10

Connecting the letter ب :

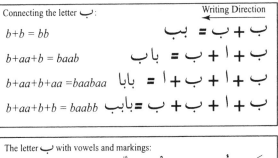

Writing Direction

$b+b = bb$ ب + ب = بب

$b+aa+b = baab$ ب + ا + ب = باب

$b+aa+b+aa = baabaa$ ب + ا + ب + ا = بابا

$b+aa+b+b = baabb$ ب + ا + ب + ب = بابب

The letter ب with vowels and markings:

بي	بو	با	بْ	بْ	بِ	بُ	بَ
bii	buu	baa	b-b	b	bi	bu	ba

The letter ب in combination with other letters:

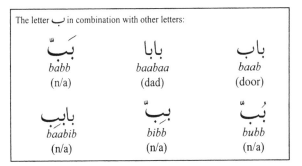

بَبّ
babb
(n/a)

بابا
baabaa
(dad)

باب
baab
(door)

بابِب
baabib
(n/a)

بِبّ
bibb
(n/a)

بُبّ
bubb
(n/a)

The letter ب in various calligraphic styles:

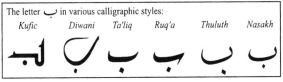

Kufic	Diwani	Ta'liq	Ruq'a	Thuluth	Nasakh

لٮٮ   ب   ٮ   ب   ب

11

Letter Name: *taa*

Transliteration: t

Pronunciation: t as in take

The letter **taa** is the 3rd letter of

ت	*taa*	تاء

the alphabet. It is a connector letter with 4 shapes. It is similar in shape to ب but with 2 dots placed over it. In handwriting, the dots can be replaced with a horizontal dash.

Examples	Location / Position / Connection	Shape / Form
بات	Isolated / Independent Not connected to any letter	ت
تاب	Initial / Beginning Connected only to following letter	تـ...
بَتا	Medial / Middle Connected to following and preceding letters	...ـتـ...
بَت	Final / End Connected only to preceding letter	ـت...

Printed form in standard script

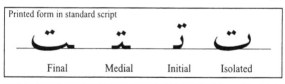

| Final | Medial | Initial | Isolated |

To write the letter, follow the arrows:

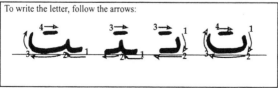

12

Connecting the letter ت :

Writing Direction ←

$b+aa+t = baat$ ب + ا + ت = بات

$t+aa+ b = taab$ ت + ا + ب = تاب

$b+t+aa+b = bataat$ ب + ت + ا + ت = بَتات

$t+aa+b+t = taabat$ ت + ا + ب + ت = تابَت

The letter ت with vowels and markings:

تي	تو	تا	تّ	تْ	تِ	تُ	تَ
tii	tuu	taa	t-t	t	ti	tu	ta

The letter ت in combination with other letters:

باتَت	باتَ	تابَت	تابَ
baatat	baata	taabat	taaba
(she was)	(to be)	(she repented)	(to repent)

تُبتُ	تُب	تَبات	تَبَّ
tubtu	tub	tabaat	tabba
(I repented)	(n/a)	(n/a)	(to perish)

The letter ت in various calligraphic styles:

Kufic	Diwani	Ta'liq	Ruq'a	Thuluth	Nasakh

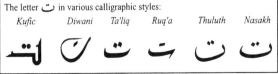

13

Letter Name: *thaa*

Transliteration: th

Pronunciation: th as in thin

ثاء *thaa* ث

The letter *thaa* is the 4th letter of the alphabet. It is a connector letter with 4 shapes. It is similar in shape to ب & ت but with 3 dots placed over it. In handwriting, the dots can be replaced with a caret (tent) shape.

Examples	Location / Position / Connection	Shape / Form
باث	Isolated / Independent Not connected to any letter	ث
ثاب	Initial / Beginning Connected only to following letter	ثـ ...
تَثبُت	Medial / Middle Connected to following and preceding letters	... ـثـ ...
تَبُث	Final / End Connected only to preceding letter	ـث ...

Printed form in standard script

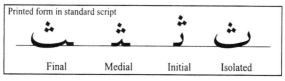

Final	Medial	Initial	Isolated

To write the letter, follow the arrows:

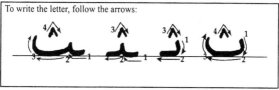

Connecting the letter ث :

Writing Direction ←

th+aa+b = thaab   ث + ا + ب = ثاب

t+th+b+t = tathbut   ت + ث + ب + ت = تَثْبُت

b+th+aa+th = bathaath   ب + ث + ا + ث = بَثاث

th+aa+b+t = thaabat   ث + ا + ب + ت = ثابَت

The letter ث with vowels and markings:

thii	thuu	thaa	th-th	th	thi	thu	tha
ثِي	ثُو	ثا	ثّ	ثْ	ثِ	ثُ	ثَ

The letter ث in combination with other letters:

بَثَّ	ثابِت	ثَبَتَ	ثاب
bath-tha	thaabit	thabata	thaab
(to broadcast)	(stationary)	(to be firm)	(n/a)

ثَبات	ثَبَّتَ	تُثْبِت	تَثْبُت
thabaat	thabbata	tuthbit	tathbut
(firmness)	(to fix)	(to prove)	(to be fixed)

The letter ث in various calligraphic styles:

Kufic	Diwani	Ta'liq	Ruq'a	Thuluth	Nasakh

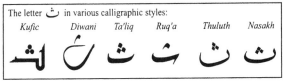

Letter Name: *jiim*

Transliteration: j

Pronunciation: j as in joke

ج

jiim   جيم

The letter *jiim* is the 5th letter of the alphabet. It is a connector letter with 4 shapes. In most of the Arab world, it is pronounced **j** as in **J**ack. In the Egyptian dialect, the *jiim* is pronounced **g** as in **g**ame.

Examples	Location / Position / Connection	Shape / Form
باج	Isolated / Independent Not connected to any letter	ج
جاب	Initial / Beginning Connected only to following letter	...ج
يجب	Medial / Middle Connected to following and preceding letters	...ج...
بيج	Final / End Connected only to preceding letter	ج...

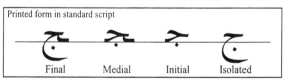

Printed form in standard script

Final   Medial   Initial   Isolated

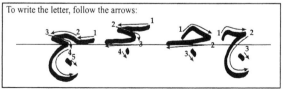

To write the letter, follow the arrows:

16

Connecting the letter ج :

Writing Direction

j+aa+b = jaab   ج + ا + ب = جاب

t+j+uu+b = tajuub   ت + ج + و + ب = تَجوب

t+aa+j = taaj   ت + ا + ج = تاج

b+ii+j = biij   ب + ي + ج = بيج

The letter ج with vowels and markings:

جي	جو	جا	جّ	جْ	جِ	جُ	جَ
jii	juu	jaa	j-j	j	ji	ju	ja

The letter ج in combination with other letters:

تَجاوُب	تاج	جَواب	جابَ
tajaawub	taaj	jawaab	jaaba
(agreement)	(crown)	(answer)	(to tour)

جُيوب	جَيب	يَجِب	جاوَبَ
juyuub	jayb	yajib	jaawaba
(pockets)	(pocket)	(must)	(he answered)

The letter ج in various calligraphic styles:

Kufic	Diwani	Ta'liq	Ruq'a	Thuluth	Nasakh

17

Letter Name: *Haa*
Transliteration: H
Pronunciation: This has no
English equivalent. It is a sound

حاء *Haa* ح

produced deep in the throat with the mouth wide open. It is close
to the sound produced when someone breathes to clean his/her
glasses. *Haa* is the 6th letter, and a connector letter with 4
shapes. It is similar in shape to ج but with no dots.

Examples	Location / Position / Connection	Shape / Form
باح	Isolated / Independent Not connected to any letter	ح
حاب	Initial / Beginning Connected only to following letter	ح...
يحب	Medial / Middle Connected to following and preceding letters	...ح...
بيح	Final / End Connected only to preceding letter	ح...

Printed form in standard script

ح	ح	ح	ح
Final	Medial	Initial	Isolated

To write the letter, follow the arrows:

18

Connecting the letter ح : **Writing Direction** ←

$H+b+ii+b = Habiib$ ح + ب + ي + ب = حبيب

$H+j+aa+b = Hijaab$ ح + ج + ا + ب = حجاب

$b+H+th = baHth$ ب + ح + ث = بحث

$t+b+ii+H = tabiiH$ ت + ب + ي + ح = تبيح

The letter ح with vowels and markings:

حي	حو	حا	حّ	حْ	حِ	حُ	حَ
Hii	Huu	Haa	H-H	H	Hi	Hu	Ha

The letter ح in combination with other letters:

بُحوث	باحِث	يَبحَث	بَحْث
buHuuth	baHith	yabHath	baHth
(researches)	(researcher)	(to research)	(research)

حُجّاج	حَبيب	تَحْت	حِجاب
Hujjaaj	Habiib	taHt	Hijaab
(pilgrims)	(beloved)	(under)	(veil)

The letter ح in various calligraphic styles:

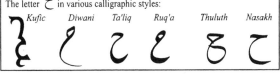

Kufic   Diwani   Ta'liq   Ruq'a   Thuluth   Nasakh

Letter Name: *khaa*
Transliteration: kh
Pronunciation: kh

خاء   *khaa*   خ

The letter *khaa* is the 7th letter of the alphabet. It is a connector letter with 4 shapes. It has no English equivalent and is pronounced as the Russian *x* or the German *ch*. It is similar in shape to ج & ح but with one dot placed over the letter.

Examples	Location / Position / Connection	Shape / Form
باخ	Isolated / Independent Not connected to any letter	خ
خاب	Initial / Beginning Connected only to following letter	خـ...
بَخت	Medial / Middle Connected to following and preceding letters	...ـخـ...
تَبيخ	Final / End Connected only to preceding letter	ـخ...

Printed form in standard script

خ   خ   خ   خ

Final   Medial   Initial   Isolated

To write the letter, follow the arrows:

20

Connecting the letter خ :

Writing Direction ←

$t+kh+t = takht$ ت + خ + ت = تَخت

$kh+aa+b+t = khaabat$ خ + ا + ب + ت = خابَت

$b+uu+kh = buukh$ ب + و + خ = بوخ

$t+j+kh = tajukh$ ت + ج + خ = تَجُخ

The letter خ with vowels and markings:

خي	خو	خا	خّ	خْ	خِ	خُ	خَ
khii	khuu	khaa	kh-kh	kh	khi	khu	kha

The letter خ in combination with other letters:

خَوْخ	بَخْت	تَخْت	يَخْت
khawkh	bakht	takht	yakht
(peach)	(luck)	(bed)	(yacht)

أُخت	أخي	أَخ	خَبيث
'ukht	'akhii	'akh	khabiith
(sister)	(my brother)	(brother)	(wicked)

The letter خ in various calligraphic styles:

Kufic   Diwani   Ta'liq   Ruq'a   Thuluth   Nasakh

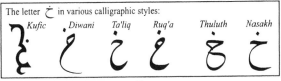

Symbol Name: *hamza*
Transliteration: ', 'a, 'u, 'i
Pronunciation: Glottal Stop, a, u, i

The *hamza* is a special sign that is not part of the Arabic alphabet. As mentioned before, the *alif* at the beginning of a word is always a seat for it. The *hamza* (ء) takes the sound of its vowel (a, u, i). Its location varies. It is written above or below the *alif* at the beginning of a word, and on the *alif* at the word's middle or end, as long as it's not followed or preceded by a vowel. When the *hamza* appears at the middle or end of a word, it may be by itself or above a *yaa* (called *kursi yaa*) or above a *waaw* (called *kursi waaw*). The *yaa* and *waaw* letters serve as seats for the *hamza*. When the *yaa* is a seat for the *hamza*, it loses its dots. In this guide, the apostrophe (') is used to indicate the *hamza* presence. For more on the *hamza*, see page 70.

Examples	Location / Position / Connection	Shape / Form
باء	Isolated / Independent / No Seat / When following a long vowel *alif*	ء
أَب	The *hamza* with *alif* seat & *fat-Ha* vowel Can be Initial, Medial or Final	ﺄ أ أَ
أُخت	The *hamza* with *alif* seat & *Damma* vowel Can be Initial, Medial or Final	أُ
إثبات	The *hamza* with *alif* seat & *kasra* vowel Can be Initial, Medial or Final	أ إ إِ

22

Examples	Location / Position / Connection	Shape / Form
جُؤب	The *hamza* with a *waaw* seat (*kursi waaw*) at the middle or end of a word, when preceded or followed by a *Damma* or long vowel *uu* (و)	ؤ ...ؤ
خَائِب	The *hamza* with a *yaa* seat (*kursi yaa*) at the middle or end of a word, when preceded or followed by a *kasra* or long vowel *ii* (ي). Since the *yaa* is a connector letter, the *hamza* will be written over any of the 4 shapes	ئ ...ئ ...ئـ... ـئـ...ى

To write the shape, follow the arrows:	Printed form in standard script
ع (with numbers 1, 2 and arrow)	ع

The *hamza* (ع) within words:

alif-hamza	أبي *'abii* (my father)	إثبات *'ithbaat* (proof)	أُخت *'ukht* (sister)	أخ *'akh* (brother)
Names of letters ending with hamza	خاء *khaa'*	حاء *Haa'*	ثاء *thaa'*	تاء *taa'*	باء *baa'*

23

Letter Name: *daal*
Transliteration: d
Pronunciation: d as in day
The letter *dhaal* is the 8th letter

دال | *daal*

of the alphabet. It is a non-connector letter with 2 shapes that rests on the base line.

Examples	Location / Position / Connection	Shape / Form
داب	Isolated / Independent / Initial Not connected to any letter	د
جَديد	Medial / Final / End Connected to preceding letter	ـد...

Printed form in standard script

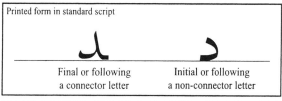

| Final or following
a connector letter | Initial or following
a non-connector letter |

To write the letter, follow the arrows:

The letter د with vowels and markings:

دي	دو	دا	دّ	دْ	دِ	دُ	دَ
dii	duu	daa	d-d	d	di	du	da

24

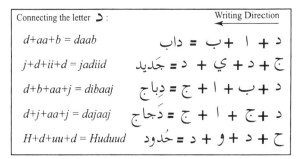

Connecting the letter **د** :

Writing Direction ←

d+aa+b = daab   د + ا + ب = داب

j+d+ii+d = jadiid   ج + د + ي + د = جَديد

d+b+aa+j = dibaaj   د + ب + ا + ج = دِباج

d+j+aa+j = dajaaj   د + ج + ا + ج = دَجاج

H+d+uu+d = Huduud   ح + د + و + د = حُدود

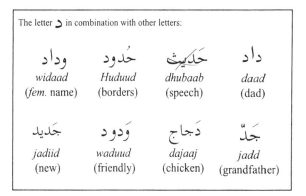

The letter **د** in combination with other letters:

داد	حَديث	حُدود	وداد
daad	dhubaab	Huduud	widaad
(dad)	(speech)	(borders)	(fem. name)

جَدّ	دَجاج	وَدود	جَديد
jadd	dajaaj	waduud	jadiid
(grandfather)	(chicken)	(friendly)	(new)

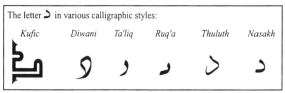

The letter **د** in various calligraphic styles:

Kufic	Diwani	Ta'liq	Ruq'a	Thuluth	Nasakh

Letter Name: *dhaal*
Transliteration: dh
Pronunciation: th as in this
The letter *dhaal* is the 9th letter

dhaal   ذ   ذال

of the alphabet. It is a non-connector letter with 2 shapes. It is similar in shape to **د**, but with one dot placed over it.

Examples	Location / Position / Connection	Shape / Form
ذاب	Isolated / Independent / Initial Not connected to any letter	ذ
جَذَب	Medial / Final / End Connected to preceding letter	ـذ...

Printed form in standard script

ـذ   ذ

Final or following a connector letter	Initial or following a non-connector letter

To write the letter, follow the arrows:

ـذ   ذ

The letter **ذ** with vowels and markings:

ذَ	ذُ	ذِ	ذْ	ذّ	ذِ	ذا	ذو	ذي
dhii	dhuu	dhaa	dh-dh	dh	dhi	dhu	dha	

26

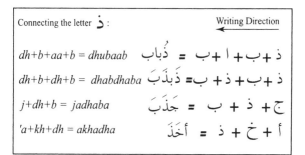

Connecting the letter ذ :

Writing Direction ←

dh+b+aa+b = dhubaab   ذ + ب + ا + ب = ذُباب

dh+b+dh+b = dhabdhaba   ذ + ب + ذ + ب = ذَبذَبَ

j+dh+b = jadhaba   ج + ذ + ب = جَذَبَ

'a+kh+dh = akhadha   أ + خ + ذ = أخَذَ

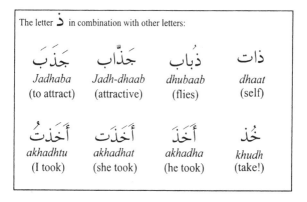

The letter ذ in combination with other letters:

جَذَبَ	جَذّاب	ذُباب	ذات
Jadhaba	Jadh-dhaab	dhubaab	dhaat
(to attract)	(attractive)	(flies)	(self)

أخَذتُ	أخَذَت	أخَذَ	خُذ
akhadhtu	akhadhat	akhadha	khudh
(I took)	(she took)	(he took)	(take!)

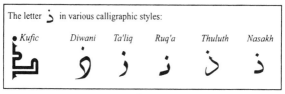

The letter ذ in various calligraphic styles:

Kufic   Diwani   Ta'liq   Ruq'a   Thuluth   Nasakh

27

Letter Name: *raa*
Transliteration: r
Pronunciation: r as in real
The letter *raa* is the 10th letter

راء | ر | *raa*

of the alphabet. It is a non-connector letter with 2 shapes. The sound is similar to Spanish "rolled" *r*.

Examples	Location / Position / Connection	Shape / Form
زار	Isolated / Independent / Initial Not connected to any letter	ر
حَجَر	Medial / Final / End Connected to preceding letter	ر...

Printed form in standard script

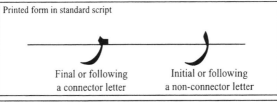

Final or following   Initial or following
a connector letter   a non-connector letter

To write the letter, follow the arrows:

The letter ر with vowels and markings:

رِي	رُو	رَا	رّ	رْ	رِ	رُ	رَ
rii	*ruu*	*raa*	*r-r*	*r*	*ri*	*ru*	*ra*

Connecting the letter ر :   Writing Direction ⟵

$d+aa+r = daar$ د + ا + ر = دار

$r+aa+d+y+uu = raadyuu$ ر + ا + د + ي + و = راديو

$H+j+r = Hajar$ ح + ج + ر = حَجَر

$j+r+j+ii+r = jarjiir$ ج + ر + ج + ي + ر = جَرجير

The letter ر in combination with other letters:

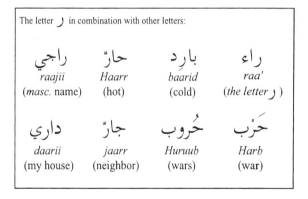

راجي
raajii
(*masc.* name)

حارّ
Haarr
(hot)

بارِد
baarid
(cold)

راء
raa'
(*the letter* ر)

داري
daarii
(my house)

جارّ
jaarr
(neighbor)

حُروب
Huruub
(wars)

حَرْب
Harb
(war)

The letter ر in various calligraphic styles:

Kufic	Diwani	Ta'liq	Ruq'a	Thuluth	Nasakh

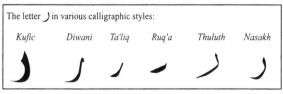

Letter Name: *zaay*
Transliteration: z
Pronunciation: z as in zeal

زاي | *zaay* ز

The letter *zaay* is the 11th letter of the alphabet. It is a non-connector letter with 2 shapes. It is similar in shape to ر, but with one dot placed over it.

Examples	Location / Position / Connection	Shape / Form
بازار	Isolated / Independent / Initial Not connected to any letter	ز
جَزَر	Medial / Final / End Connected to preceding letter	...ـز

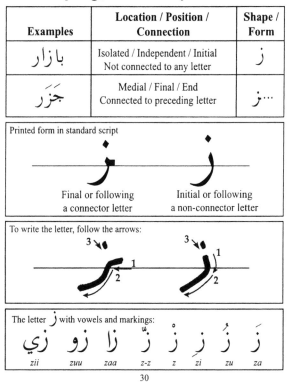

Printed form in standard script

Final or following a connector letter — Initial or following a non-connector letter

To write the letter, follow the arrows:

The letter ز with vowels and markings:

زَي زو زا زّ زْ زِ زُ زَ
zii zuu zaa z-z z zi zu za

30

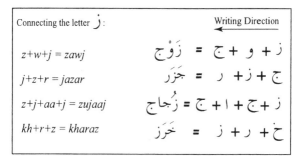

Connecting the letter ز :

Writing Direction ←

$z+w+j = zawj$ زَوْج = ج + و + ز

$j+z+r = jazar$ جَزَر = ر + ز + ج

$z+j+aa+j = zujaaj$ زُجاج = ج + ا + ج + ز

$kh+r+z = kharaz$ خَرَز = ز + ر + خ

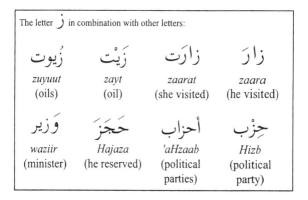

The letter ز in combination with other letters:

زُيوت	زَيْت	زارَت	زارَ
zuyuut	zayt	zaarat	zaara
(oils)	(oil)	(she visited)	(he visited)

وَزير	حَجَزَ	أحزاب	حِزْب
waziir	Hajaza	'aHzaab	Hizb
(minister)	(he reserved)	(political parties)	(political party)

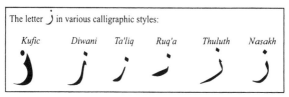

The letter ز in various calligraphic styles:

Kufic	Diwani	Ta'liq	Ruq'a	Thuluth	Nasakh

Letter Name: *siin*
Transliteration: s
Pronunciation: s as in snake
The letter *siin* is the 12th letter

سين
س
siin

of the alphabet. It is a connector letter with 4 shapes. In
handwriting, the teeth of the *siin* are not normally written.

Examples	Location / Position / Connection	Shape / Form
راس	Isolated / Independent Not connected to any letter	س
ساد	Initial / Beginning Connected only to following letter	سـ...
حَسَب	Medial / Middle Connected to following and preceding letters	...ـسـ...
يابِس	Final / End Connected only to preceding letter	ـس...

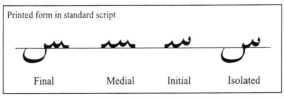

Printed form in standard script

Final   Medial   Initial   Isolated

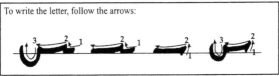

To write the letter, follow the arrows:

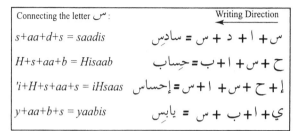

ا ب ت ث ج ح خ د ذ ر ز س ش ص ض ط ظ ع غ ف ق ك ل م ن هـ و ي

Connecting the letter س :

Writing Direction ←

s+aa+d+s = saadis	س + ا + د + س = سادِس
H+s+aa+b = Hisaab	ح + س + ا + ب = حِساب
'i+H+s+aa+s = iHsaas	إ + ح + س + ا + س = إحساس
y+aa+b+s = yaabis	ي + ا + ب + س = يابِس

The letter س with vowels and markings:

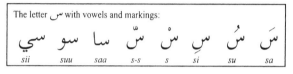

سِي | سُو | سَا | سّ | سْ | سِ | سُ | سَ
sii | suu | saa | s-s | s | si | su | sa

The letter س in combination with other letters:

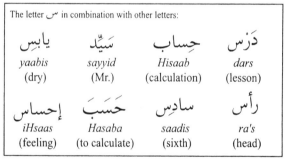

يابِس	سَيِّد	حِساب	دَرس
yaabis	sayyid	Hisaab	dars
(dry)	(Mr.)	(calculation)	(lesson)

إحساس	حَسَبَ	سادِس	رأس
iHsaas	Hasaba	saadis	ra's
(feeling)	(to calculate)	(sixth)	(head)

The letter س in various calligraphic styles:

Kufic | Diwani | Ta'liq | Ruq'a | Thuluth | Nasakh

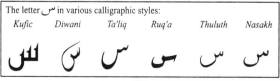

33

Letter Name: *shiin*
Transliteration: sh
Pronunciation: sh as in shake

شين *shiin* ش

The letter *shiin* is the 13th letter of the alphabet. It is a connector letter with 4 shapes and is similar in shape to *siin* (س), but with 3 dots placed over it.

Examples	Location / Position / Connection	Shape / Form
داش	Isolated / Independent Not connected to any letter	ش
شَيخ	Initial / Beginning Connected only to following letter	شـ...
بَشَر	Medial / Middle Connected to following and preceding letters	...شـ...
جَيش	Final / End Connected only to preceding letter	ـش...

Printed form in standard script

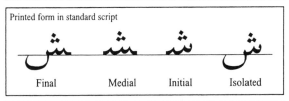

Final　　　Medial　　　Initial　　　Isolated

To write the letter, follow the arrows:

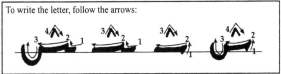

34

Connecting the letter ش :

Writing Direction ←

sh+d+ii+d = shadiid ‎ش + د + ي + د = شَديد

y+sh+kh+r = yashkhur ‎ي + ش + خ + ر = يَشخُر

r+sh+aa+d = rashaad ‎ر + ش + ا + د = رَشاد

H+sh+ii+sh = Hashiish ‎ح + ش + ي + ش = حَشيش

The letter ش with vowels and markings:

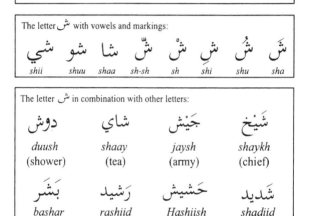

شِي	شُو	شا	شّ	شْ	شِ	شُ	شَ
shii	shuu	shaa	sh-sh	sh	shi	shu	sha

The letter ش in combination with other letters:

دوش	شاي	جَيش	شَيخ
duush	shaay	jaysh	shaykh
(shower)	(tea)	(army)	(chief)

بَشَر	رَشيد	حَشيش	شَديد
bashar	rashiid	Hashiish	shadiid
(people)	(masc. name)	(grass)	(strong)

The letter ش in various calligraphic styles:

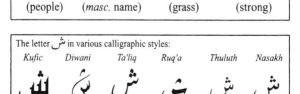

Kufic	Diwani	Ta'liq	Ruq'a	Thuluth	Nasakh

Letter Name: *Saad*
Transliteration: S
Pronunciation: S (*emphatic*)

	صاد	ص
	Saad	

The sound for the letter ***Saad*** is produced further back in the mouth. It also gives the surrounding a deeper sound. ***Saad*** is the 14th letter of the alphabet and is a connector letter with 4 shapes.

Examples	Location / Position / Connection	Shape / Form
باص	Isolated / Independent Not connected to any letter	ص
صاحِب	Initial / Beginning Connected only to following letter	صـ...
تَصدُر	Medial / Middle Connected to following and preceding letters	...ـصـ...
رَخيص	Final / End Connected only to preceding letter	ـص...

Printed form in standard script

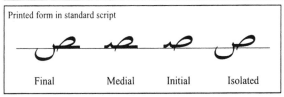

Final   Medial   Initial   Isolated

To write the letter, follow the arrows:

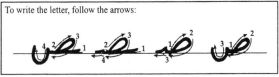

36

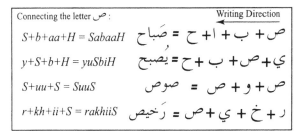

ا ب ت ث ج ح خ د ذ ر ز س ش ص **ض** ط ظ ع غ ف ق ك ل م ن ه و ي

Connecting the letter ص :

Writing Direction ←

ص + ب + ا + ح = صَباح   S+b+aa+H = SabaaH

ي + ص + ب + ح = يصبح   y+S+b+H = yuSbiH

ص + و + ص = صوص   S+uu+S = SuuS

ر + خ + ي + ص = رَخيص   r+kh+ii+S = rakhiiS

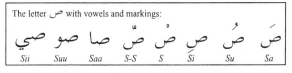

The letter ص with vowels and markings:

صَ   صُ   صِ   صْ   صّ   صا   صو   صي

Sa   Su   Si   S   S-S   Saa   Suu   Sii

The letter ص in combination with other letters:

صاد   صاحِب   صَباح   باص

Saad   SaaHib   SabaaH   baaS

(the letter ص)   (friend)   (morning)   (bus)

تَصوير   رَخيص   صورة   صَحيح

taSwiir   rakhiiS   Suura   SaHiiH

(photography)   (cheap)   (picture)   (correct)

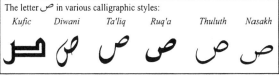

The letter ص in various calligraphic styles:

Kufic   Diwani   Ta'liq   Ruq'a   Thuluth   Nasakh

صـ   ص   ص   ص   ص   صـ

Letter Name: *Daad*
Transliteration: D
Pronunciation: D (*emphatic*)

The letter ***Daad*** is the 15th letter
of the alphabet. It is a connector letter with 4 shapes. It is similar
in shape to ص but with a dot placed over it.

Examples	Location / Position / Connection	Shape / Form
أَرْض	Isolated / Independent Not connected to any letter	ض
ضَباب	Initial / Beginning Connected only to following letter	ضـ...
أخضَر	Medial / Middle Connected to following and preceding letters	...ـضـ...
أبيَض	Final / End Connected only to preceding letter	ـض...

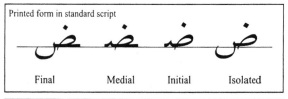

Printed form in standard script

Final　　Medial　　Initial　　Isolated

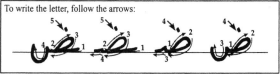

To write the letter, follow the arrows:

38

Connecting the letter ض :

Writing Direction ←

ر + ي + ا + ض = رِياض   r+y+aa+D = riyaaD

ض + ب + ا + ب = ضَباب   D+b+aa+b = Dabaab

أ + خ + ض + ر = أخضَر   'a+kh+D+r = 'akhDar

أ + ب + ي + ض = أبيَض   'a+b+y+D = 'abyaD

The letter ض with vowels and markings:

ضِي   ضُو   ضا   ضّ   ضْ   ضِ   ضُ   ضَ

Dii   Duu   Daa   D-D   D   Di   Du   Da

The letter ض in combination with other letters:

أبيَض   أخضَر   ضَرَبَ   ضاد

abyaD   akhDar   Daraba   Daad

(white)   (green)   (to strike)   (the letter ض)

رَوض   أرضي   ضَباب   بَيض

rawD   arDii   Dabaab   bayD

(meadow)   (earthly)   (fog)   (eggs)

The letter ض in various calligraphic styles:

Kufic   Diwani   Ta'liq   Ruq'a   Thuluth   Nasakh

39

ط ظ ع غ ف ق ك ل م ن ه و ي ا ب ت ث ج ح خ د ذ ر ز س ش ص ض

Letter Name: *Taa*
Transliteration: T
Pronunciation: T (*emphatic*)
The sound of the letter *Taa* is

Taa طاء

produced further back in the mouth. It is the 16th letter of the alphabet. It is a connector letter with 4 shapes. It is similar in shape to the initial *Saad* ص but with a vertical stroke.

Examples	Location / Position / Connection	Shape / Form
رِباط	Isolated / Independent Not connected to any letter	ط
طَبيب	Initial / Beginning Connected only to following letter	...ط
يَطير	Medial / Middle Connected to following and preceding letters	...ط...
بَطّ	Final / End Connected only to preceding letter	ط...

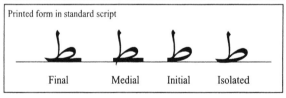

Printed form in standard script

Final　Medial　Initial　Isolated

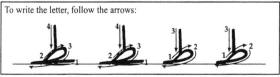

To write the letter, follow the arrows:

40

Connecting the letter ط :　　　　　　　　**← Writing Direction**

$T+b+ii+b = Tabiib$　　ط + ب + ي + ب = طَبيب

$r+b+aa+T = ribaaT$　　ر + ب + ا + ط = رباط

$y+T+ii+r = yaTiir$　　ي + ط + ي + ر = يَطير

$kh+T+uu+T = khuTuuT$　　خ + ط + و + ط = خُطوط

The letter ط with vowels and markings:

طِي　طُو　طا　طّ　طْ　طِ　طُ　طَ

Tii　Tuu　Taa　T-T　T　Ti　Tu　Ta

The letter ط in combination with other letters:

شُرطِي　بَطّيخ　تَطْوير　طاء

shurTii　baTTiikh　taTwiir　Taa'
(policeman)　(melons)　(development)　(the letter ط)

طبيب　طيّار　يَطير　طار

Tabiib　Tayyaar　yaTiir　Taar
(doctor)　(pilot)　(he flies)　(to fly)

The letter ط in various calligraphic styles:

Kufic　Diwani　Ta'liq　Ruq'a　Thuluth　Nasakh

ط　ط　ط　ط　ط　ط

41

Letter Name: *DHaa*
Transliteration: DH
Pronunciation: DH (*emphatic*)

ظاء	ظ
	DHaa

The letter ***DHaa*** is the 17th letter of the alphabet. It is a connector letter with 4 shapes. It is similar in shape to ط but with a dot placed over it. In some Arabic dialects, ***DHaa*** is sometimes pronounced Z (*emphatic*).

Examples	Location / Position / Connection	Shape / Form
بوظ	Isolated / Independent Not connected to any letter	ظ
ظَبي	Initial / Beginning Connected only to following letter	ظ...
يَحظو	Medial / Middle Connected to following and preceding letters	...ظ...
حَظّ	Final / End Connected only to preceding letter	...ظ

Printed form in standard script

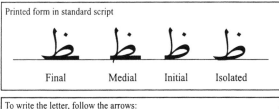

Final	Medial	Initial	Isolated

To write the letter, follow the arrows:

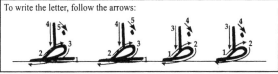

42

ا ب ت ث ج ح خ د ذ ر ز س ش ص ض ط ظ ع غ ف ق ك ل م ن ه و ي

Connecting the letter ظ :

Writing Direction

$DH+b+ii = DHabii$ ظ + ب + ي = ظَبِي

$H+DH = HaDH\text{-}DH$ ح + ظ = حَظّ

$y+H+DH+r = yaH\text{-}DHur$ ي + ح + ظ + ر = يَحْظُر

$DH+b+aa' = DHibaa'$ ظ + ب + ا + ء = ظِباء

The letter ظ with vowels and markings:

ظِي ظُو ظَا ظّ ظْ ظِ ظُ ظَ

DHii · DHuu · DHaa · DH-DH · DH · DHi · DHu · DHa

The letter ظ in combination with other letters:

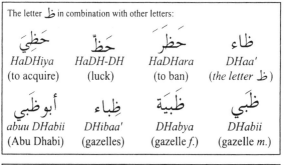

حَظِيَ — HaDHiya (to acquire)
حَظّ — HaDH-DH (luck)
حَظَرَ — HaDHara (to ban)
ظاء — DHaa' (the letter ظ)

أبو ظَبِي — abuu DHabii (Abu Dhabi)
ظِباء — DHibaa' (gazelles)
ظَبْية — DHabya (gazelle f.)
ظَبِي — DHabii (gazelle m.)

The letter ظ in various calligraphic styles:

Kufic · Diwani · Ta'liq · Ruq'a · Thuluth · Nasakh

43

Letter Name: *ᶜayn*
Transliteration: *ᶜ*
Pronunciation: The letter *ᶜayn*

عين   *ᶜayn*   ع

has no English equivalent. It is a voiced counterpart of the ح and sounds like a strangulated *ah*. The letter *ᶜayn* is the 18th letter of the alphabet. It is a connector letter with 4 shapes.

Examples	Location / Position / Connection	Shape / Form
باع	Isolated / Independent Not connected to any letter	ع
عَرَب	Initial / Beginning Connected only to following letter	ع...
يَعِيش	Medial / Middle Connected to following and preceding letters	...ع...
ضَبع	Final / End Connected only to preceding letter	ع...

Printed form in standard script

  ع   ع   ع   ع

Final   Medial   Initial   Isolated

To write the letter, follow the arrows:

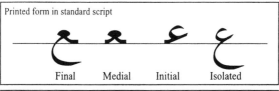

44

Connecting the letter ع :

← Writing Direction

^{c}+r+b = ^{c}*arab*   عَرَب = ب + ر + عَ

$'u$+s+b+uu+^{c} = *'usbuu*^{c} أُسبوع = ع + و + ب + س + ا

s+^{c}+uu+d = *sa*^{c}*uud*   سَعود = د + و + عـ + س

sh+aa+r+^{c} = *shaari*^{c} شارِع = عـ + ر + ا + ش

The letter ع with vowels and markings:

عي	عو	عا	عّ	عْ	عِ	عُ	عَ
^{c}*ii*	^{c}*uu*	^{c}*aa*	^{c}_^{c}	^{c}	^{c}*i*	^{c}*u*	^{c}*a*

The letter ع in combination with other letters:

ضَبع	شارِع	أُسبوع	عَرَب
Dab^c	*shaari*^{c}	*usbuu*^{c}	^{c}*arab*
(hyena)	(street)	(week)	(Arabs)

عشرة	تسعة	سبعة	اربعة
^{c}*ashara*	*tis*^{c}*a*	*sab*^{c}*a*	*arba*^{c}*a*
(ten)	(nine)	(seven)	(four)

The letter ع in various calligraphic styles:

Kufic	Diwani	Ta'liq	Ruq'a	Thuluth	Nasakh

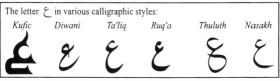

Letter Name: *ghayn*
Transliteration: gh
Pronunciation: gh

| | *ghayn* | غين |

The letter *ghayn* is the 19th letter
of the alphabet. It has no English equivalent. The sound is
similar to the throaty French *r*. It is a connector letter with 4
shapes, with a similar shape to ع but with a dot placed over it.

Examples	Location / Position / Connection	Shape / Form
صاغ	Isolated / Independent Not connected to any letter	غ
غَدير	Initial / Beginning Connected only to following letter	غـ
يَغضَب	Medial / Middle Connected to following and preceding letters	ـغـ
تَبغ	Final / End Connected only to preceding letter	ـغ

Printed form in standard script

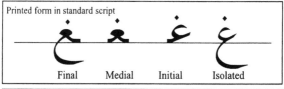

| Final | Medial | Initial | Isolated |

To write the letter, follow the arrows:

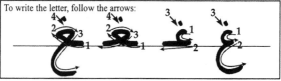

46

Connecting the letter غ :   Writing Direction →

gh+r+aa+b = ghuraab   غُراب = ب + ا + ر + غ

b+gh+d+aa+d = baghdaad   بَغداد = د + ا + د + غ + ب

gh+r+ii+b = ghariib   غَريب = ب + ي + ر + غ

t+b+gh = tabgh   تَبغ = غ + ب + ت

The letter غ with vowels and markings:

غِي	غو	غا	غّ	غْ	غِ	غُ	غَ
ghii	ghuu	ghaa	gh-gh	gh	ghi	ghu	gha

The letter غ in combination with other letters:

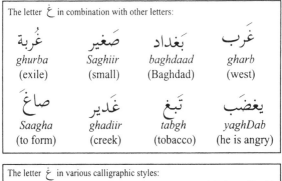

غُربة	صَغير	بَغداد	غرب
ghurba	Saghiir	baghdaad	gharb
(exile)	(small)	(Baghdad)	(west)

صاغَ	غَدير	تَبغ	يَغضَب
Saagha	ghadiir	tabgh	yaghDab
(to form)	(creek)	(tobacco)	(he is angry)

The letter غ in various calligraphic styles:

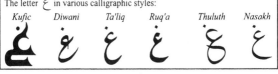

Kufic	Diwani	Ta'liq	Ruq'a	Thuluth	Nasakh

Letter Name: *faa*
Transliteration: f
Pronunciation: f as in face

فاء	*faa*	ف

The letter *faa* is the 20th letter of the alphabet. It is a connector letter with 4 shapes. The tail of the *faa* rests on the writing line.

Examples	Location / Position / Connection	Shape / Form
خَروف	Isolated / Independent Not connected to any letter	ف
فار	Initial / Beginning Connected only to following letter	ﻓ...
سَفارة	Medial / Middle Connected to following and preceding letters	...ﻔ...
سَيف	Final / End Connected only to preceding letter	...ﻒ

Printed form in standard script

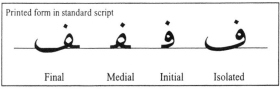

Final   Medial   Initial   Isolated

To write the letter, follow the arrows:

48

Connecting the letter ف:

Writing Direction ←

$f+r+aa+gh = faraagh$ ف + ر + ا + غ = فَرَاغ

$s+f+ii+r = safiir$ س + ف + ي + ر = سَفِير

$DH+r+f = DHarf$ ظ + ر + ف = ظَرْف

$s+y+f = sayf$ س + ي + ف = سَيْف

The letter ف with vowels and markings:

فِي	فُو	فَا	فّ	فْ	فِ	فُ	فَ
fii	fuu	faa	f-f	f	fi	fu	fa

The letter ف in combination with other letters:

عَفِيف	عَفَاف	سُيوف	فاء
ᶜafiif	ᶜafaaf	suyuuf	faa
(masc. name)	(fem. name)	(swords)	(the letter ف)

زَرَافة	ضُفدَع	فراشة	فأر
zaraafa	Dufdaᶜ	faraasha	fa'r
(giraffe)	(frog)	(butterfly)	(mouse)

The letter ف in various calligraphic styles:

Kufic	Diwani	Ta'liq	Ruq'a	Thuluth	Nasakh
ڧـ	ڤ	ف	ف	ف	ف

Letter Name: *qaaf*
Transliteration: q
Pronunciation: q (*emphatic*)

قاف   *qaaf*   ق

The letter *qaaf* is the 21st letter of the alphabet. It is a connector letter with 4 shapes. It is similar in shape to the letter ف, but with 2 dots placed over. The tail extends below the writing line.

Examples	Location / Position / Connection	Shape / Form
طارق	Isolated / Independent Not connected to any letter	ق
قفص	Initial / Beginning Connected only to following letter	ق ...
يقرأ	Medial / Middle Connected to following and preceding letters	... ـقـ ...
رفيق	Final / End Connected only to preceding letter	ق ...

Printed form in standard script

ق   ق   ـقـ   ـق

Final   Medial   Initial   Isolated

To write the letter, follow the arrows:

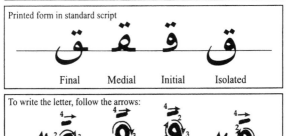

50

Connecting the letter ق:

Writing Direction ←

$q+f+S = qafaS$	ق + ف + ص = قَفَص
$T+aa+r+q = Taariq$	ط + ا + ر + ق = طارِق
$d+q+ii+q = daqiiq$	د + ق + ي + ق = دَقيق
$r+f+ii+q = rafiiq$	ر + ف + ي + ق = رَفيق

The letter ق with vowels and markings:

قي	قو	قا	قّ	قْ	قِ	قُ	قَ
qii	quu	qaa	q-q	q	qi	qu	qa

The letter ق in combination with other letters:

دقيقة	قصير	قطر	قاف
daqiiqa	qaSiir	qaTar	qaaf
(minute)	(short)	(Qatar)	(the letter ق)

شفيق	قطع	قراءة	يقرأ
shafiiq	qaTaᶜa	qiraa'a	yaqra'
(masc. name)	(to cut)	(reading)	(he reads)

The letter ق in various calligraphic styles:

Kufic	Diwani	Ta'liq	Ruq'a	Thuluth	Nasakh
ق	ق	ق	ه	ق	ق

51

Letter Name: *kaaf*
Transliteration: k
Pronunciation: k as in key

kaaf ك	كاف

The letter *kaaf* is the 22nd letter of the alphabet. It is a connector letter with 4 shapes. When the *kaaf* appears at the end of a noun, it is often a suffix meaning *your*, regardless of the noun's gender.

Examples	Location / Position / Connection	Shape / Form
جاك	Isolated / Independent Not connected to any letter	ك
كِتاب	Initial / Beginning Connected only to following letter	كـ...
يَكتُب	Medial / Middle Connected to following and preceding letters	...ـكـ...
بَيتُكَ	Final / End Connected only to preceding letter	...ـك

Printed form in standard script

ك   ك   كـ   ـك

Final   Medial   Initial   Isolated

To write the letter, follow the arrows:

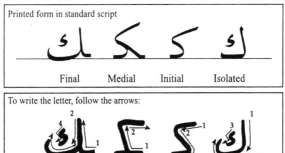

Connecting the letter ك :   Writing Direction ←

$k+t+aa+b = kitaab$ كِتاب = ب + ا + ت + ك

$k+ c + k = ka^ck$ كَعك = ك + ع + ك

$d+k+t+uu+r = daktuur$ دكتور = ر + و + ت + ك + د

$sh+k+uu+k = shukuuk$ شُكوك = ك + و + ك + ش

The letter ك with vowels and markings:

كِي	كُو	كا	كَّ	كْ	كِ	كُ	كَ
kii	kuu	kaa	k-k	k	ki	ku	ka

The letter ك in combination with other letters:

يَكسِر	كَبير	كَثير	كاف
yaksir	kabiir	kathiir	kaaf
(he breaks)	(big)	(a lot)	(*the letter* ك)

كِتابُكِ	سُكّر	كُرسي	بَيتُكَ
kitaabuki	sukkar	kursii	baytuka
(your book *f.*)	(sugar)	(seat)	(your house *m.*)

The letter ك in various calligraphic styles:

Kufic	Diwani	Ta'liq	Ruq'a	Thuluth	Nasakh

53

Letter Name: *laam*
Transliteration: l
Pronunciation: l as in leaf

The letter *laam* is the 23rd letter | *laam*
of the alphabet. It is a connector letter with 4 shapes. The *alif* (ا)
and the *laam* (ل) together form the prefix *al-* (ال), the equivalent
of the definite article *the*.

Examples	Location / Position / Connection	Shape / Form
غَزال	Isolated / Independent Not connected to any letter	ل
ليبيا	Initial / Beginning Connected only to following letter	ل...
كَلب	Medial / Middle Connected to following and preceding letters	...ل...
طَويل	Final / End Connected only to preceding letter	...ل

Printed form in standard script

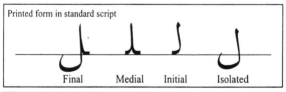

Final　　Medial　　Initial　　Isolated

To write the letter, follow the arrows:

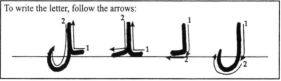

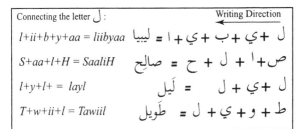

Connecting the letter ل :

Writing Direction ←

l+ii+b+y+aa = liibyaa   ل + ي + ب + ي + ا = ليبيا

S+aa+l+H = SaaliH   ص + ا + ل + ح = صالِح

l+y+l+ = layl   ل + ي + ل = لَيل

T+w+ii+l = Tawiil   ط + و + ي + ل = طَويل

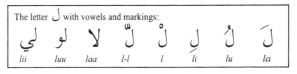

The letter ل with vowels and markings:

لي	لو	لا	لّ	لْ	لِ	لُ	لَ
lii	*luu*	*laa*	*l-l*	*l*	*li*	*lu*	*la*

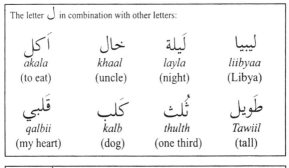

The letter ل in combination with other letters:

ليبيا	لَيلة	خال	اَكل
liibyaa	*layla*	*khaal*	*akala*
(Libya)	(night)	(uncle)	(to eat)

طَويل	ثُلث	كَلب	قَلبي
Tawiil	*thulth*	*kalb*	*qalbii*
(tall)	(one third)	(dog)	(my heart)

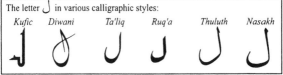

The letter ل in various calligraphic styles:

Kufic	Diwani	Ta'liq	Ruq'a	Thuluth	Nasakh

55

Letter Name: *miim*
Transliteration: m
Pronunciation: m as in make

The letter *miim* is the 24th letter

ميم | مـ | *miim*

of the alphabet. It is a connector letter with 4 shapes.

Examples	Location / Position / Connection	Shape / Form
أُمّ	Isolated / Independent Not connected to any letter	مـ
مَدرَسة	Initial / Beginning Connected only to following letter	...مـ
جَمَل	Medial / Middle Connected to following and preceding letters	...مـ...
سَليم	Final / End Connected only to preceding letter	مـ...

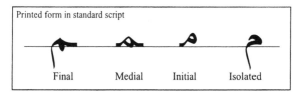

Printed form in standard script

Final   Medial   Initial   Isolated

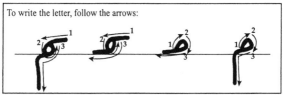

To write the letter, follow the arrows:

56

Connecting the letter م :

Writing Direction

m+d+r+s+(tied taa) = madrasa مدرسة = ة + س + ر + د + م

kh+ m+s+(tied taa) = khamsa خمسة = ة + س + م + خ

d+m+sh+q = dimashq دِمشق = ق + ش + م + د

s+l+ii+m = saliim سَليم = م + ي + ل + س

The letter م with vowels and markings:

مي   مو   ما   مّ   مْ   مِ   مُ   مَ

mii   muu   maa   m-m   m   mi   mu   ma

The letter م in combination with other letters:

كَريم   شَمس   جامِعة   جَمَل

kariim   shams   jaami‘a   jamal

(generous)   (sun)   (university)   (camel)

When م is joined to ب ت ث س ل م, it may be written like this:

سَمير   مُمتاز   المَغرِب   تَمام

samiir   mumtaaz   al-maghrib   tamaam

(masc. name)   (excellent)   (Morocco)   (perfect)

The letter م in various calligraphic styles:

Kufic	Diwani	Ta'liq	Ruq'a	Thuluth	Nasakh

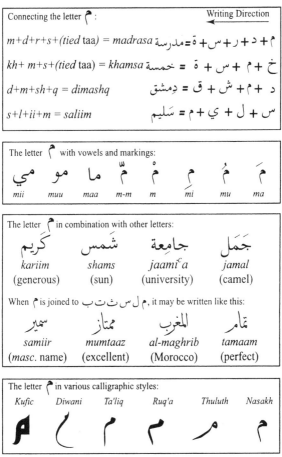

Letter Name: *nuun*
Transliteration: n
Pronunciation: n as in none

	نون	ن
	nuun	

The letter ***nuun*** is the 25th letter of the alphabet. It is a connector letter with 4 shapes. The initial and medial forms of ن are similar in shape to ب but with the dot placed over it rather than below.

Examples	Location / Position / Connection	Shape / Form
لَيمون	Isolated / Independent Not connected to any letter	ن
نار	Initial / Beginning Connected only to following letter	نـ ...
كَنَدا	Medial / Middle Connected to following and preceding letters	... ـنـ ...
تَمرين	Final / End Connected only to preceding letter	ـن...

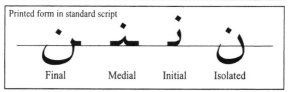

Printed form in standard script

Final   Medial   Initial   Isolated

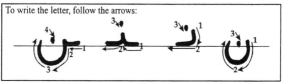

To write the letter, follow the arrows:

Connecting the letter ن :

Writing Direction ←

$n + uu + r = nuur$ ن + و + ر = نور

$b+n+aa+y+(tied\ taa)= binaaya$ ب + ن + ا + ي + ة = بِناية

$l+b+n+aa+n = lubnaan$ ل + ب + ن + ا + ن = لُبنان

$f+l+s+T+ii+n = filasTiin$ ف + ل + س + ط + ي + ن = فِلَسطين

The letter ن with vowels and markings:

نِي	نو	نا	نّ	نْ	نِ	نُ	نَ
nii	nuu	naa	n-n	n	ni	nu	na

The letter ن in combination with other letters:

نَحنُ	أنتِ	أنتَ	أنا
naHnu	anti	anta	anaa
(we)	(you f.)	(you m.)	(I)

عَمّان	اليمن	عُمان	تونس
ᶜammaan	al-yaman	ᶜumaan	tuunis
(Amman)	(Yemen)	(Oman)	(Tunisia)

The letter ن in various calligraphic styles:

Kufic	Diwani	Ta'liq	Ruq'a	Thuluth	Nasakh

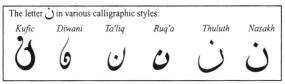

59

Letter Name: *haa*
Transliteration: h
Pronunciation: h as in hat

هاء *haa*

The letter *haa* is the 26th letter of the alphabet. It is a connector letter with 4 shapes. The shape of the isolated and final *haa* is the same as the *taa marbuuTa*, but without the dots. Generally, the *haa* at the end of a word is the equivalent of the English *his*.

Examples	Location / Position / Connection	Shape / Form
أباه	Isolated / Independent Not connected to any letter	ه
هَرَم	Initial / Beginning Connected only to following letter	هـ ...
كِتابُها	Medial / Middle Connected to following and preceding letters	... ـهـ ...
كِتابُهُ	Final / End Connected only to preceding letter	ـه ...

Printed form in standard script

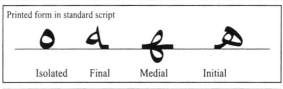

Isolated   Final   Medial   Initial

To write the letter, follow the arrows:

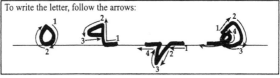

60

Connecting the letter هـ :

Writing Direction →

$h+w+aa+' = hawaa'$ هـ + و + ا + ء = هَوَاء

$s+h+y+l = suhayl$ س+ هـ +ي +ل = سُهَيل

$k+t+aa+b+h+aa = kitaabuhaa$ ك +ت +ا +ب +هـ = كِتَابُها

$k+t+aa+b+h = kitaabuhu$ ك +ت +ا +ب +هـ = كِتَابُهُ

The letter هـ with vowels and markings:

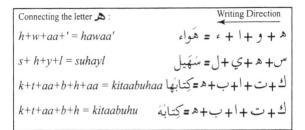

هِي	هُو	هَا	هّ	هْ	هِ	هُ	هَ
hii	huu	haa	h-h	h	hi	hu	ha

The letter هـ in combination with other letters:

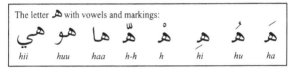

هُم	هِيَ	هُوَ	هَاء
hum	hiya	huwa	haa'
(they)	(she)	(he)	(the letter هـ)

كِتَابُهم	كِتَابُها	كِتَابُهُ	الله
kitaabuhum	kitaabuhaa	kitabuhu	allah
(their book)	(her book)	(his book)	(God)

The initial, medial, and final letter هـ in various calligraphic styles:

Kufic   *Diwani*   *Ta'liq*   *Ruq'a*   *Thuluth*   *Nasakh*

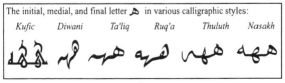

Letter Name: *waaw*
Transliteration: **w** (consonant)
   or **uu** (as a long vowel)
Pronunciation: **w** as in **w**ake
   or **oo** as in m**oo**n

واو   *waaw*   و

The letter *waaw* is the 27th letter of the alphabet. It has two functions: a long vowel pronounced **oo** as in m**oo**n, and a consonant pronounced **w** as in **w**ake when at the beginning of a word, followed, or preceded by a short or long vowel. It is a non-connector letter with 2 shapes. When *waaw* is attached to a word that follows it, it means *and*.

Examples	Location / Position / Connection	Shape / Form
واو	Isolated / Independent / Initial Not connected to any letter	و
توت	Medial / Final / End Connected to preceding letter	و...

Printed form in standard script

و   و

Final or following a connector letter

Initial or following a non-connector letter

To write the letter, follow the arrows:

Connecting the letter **و** :
Writing Direction ←

t+uu+t = *tuut*	ت + و + ت = توت
b+uu+t = *buut*	ب + و + ت = بوت
w+aa+th+b = *waathib*	و + ا + ث + ب = واثِب
t+aa+b+uu+t = *taabuut*	ت + ا + ب + و + ت = تابوت

The letter **و** with vowels and markings:

وي	وو	وا	وّ	وْ	وِ	وُ	وَ
wii	*wuu*	*waa*	*w-w*	*w*	*wi*	*wu*	*wa*

The letter **و** in combination with other letters:

ثُبوت	تابوت	ثَواب	بَوّاب
thubuut	*taabuut*	*thawaab*	*bawwaab*
(steadiness)	(coffin)	(reward)	(doorman)

ثَوب	وَثَبَ	او	واو
thawb	*wathaba*	*aw*	*waaw*
(dress)	(to jump)	(or)	(*the letter* **و**)

The letter **و** in various calligraphic styles:

Kufic	Diwani	Ta'liq	Ruq'a	Thuluth	Nasakh
ﭸ	**ر**	**و**	**و**	**و**	**و**

63

Letter Name: *yaa*
Transliteration: y (consonant)
or ii (as a vowel)
Pronunciation: y as in yell
or ee as in beet

The letter *yaa* is the 28th and last letter of the alphabet. It has two functions: a long vowel **ii** pronounced **ee** as in b**ee**t, and a consonant pronounced **y** as in **y**ell when at the beginning of a word, followed, or preceded by a short or long vowel. It is a connector letter with 4 shapes.

Examples	Location / Position / Connection	Shape / Form
باوي	Isolated / Independent Not connected to any letter	ي
يَبيت	Initial / Beginning Connected only to following letter	... يـ
تَبيت	Medial / Middle Connected to following and preceding letters	... يـ ...
بابي	Final / End Connected only to preceding letter	ي ...

Printed form in standard script

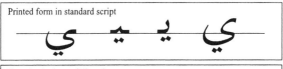

To write the letter, follow the arrows:

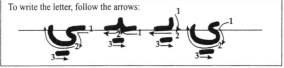

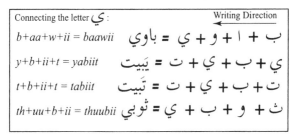

Connecting the letter ي :

Writing Direction →

b+aa+w+ii = baawii ب + ا + و + ي = باوي

y+b+ii+t = yabiit ي + ب + ي + ت = يَبيت

t+b+ii+t = tabiit ت + ب + ي + ت = تَبيت

th+uu+b+ii = thuubii ث + و + ب + ي = ثُوبي

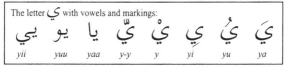

The letter ي with vowels and markings:

يَ	يُ	يِ	يّ	يْ	يِ	يُ	يِي	يو
yii	yuu	yaa	y-y	y	yi	yu	ya	

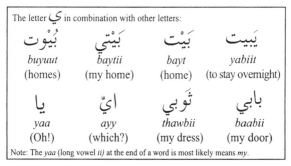

The letter ي in combination with other letters:

بُيُوت	بَيْتي	بَيْت	يَبيت
buyuut	baytii	bayt	yabiit
(homes)	(my home)	(home)	(to stay overnight)

يا	ايّ	ثَوبي	بابي
yaa	ayy	thawbii	baabii
(Oh!)	(which?)	(my dress)	(my door)

Note: The *yaa* (long vowel *ii*) at the end of a word is most likely means *my*.

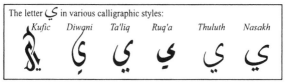

The letter ي in various calligraphic styles:

Kufic	Diwani	Ta'liq	Ruq'a	Thuluth	Nasakh
ي	ي	ي	ي	ي	ي

تاء مربوطة   *taa marbuuTa*

Symbol Name: *taa marbuuTa*

The *taa marbuuTa* (*lit.* tied *taa*) is not part of the Arabic alphabet. It is a grammatical symbol that occurs only at the end of a word to indicate that the word's gender is feminine (with a few exceptions). It comes in two shapes. It is pronounced as a *fat-Ha* (short vowel *a*), and sometimes as a regular *taa* (ت) when followed by a suffix, such as possessive pronouns.

Examples	Location / Position / Connection	Shape / Form
سيارة	Final / End Not connected to preceding letter	ة
زوجة	Final / End Connected to preceding letter	...ة

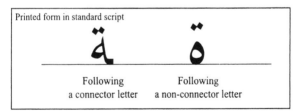

Printed form in standard script

Following a connector letter   Following a non-connector letter

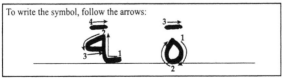

To write the symbol, follow the arrows:

66

Connecting the shape ة : ← Writing Direction

s+y+d+(*tied* taa) = *sayyida* سَيِّدة = ة + د + يّ + س

j+r+ii+d+(*tied* taa) = *jariida* جَريدة = ة + د + ي + ر + ج

d+j+aa+j+(*tied* taa) = *dajaaja* دَجاجة = ة + ج+ا+ج+د

d+r+aa+s+(*tied* taa) = *diraasa* دِراسة = ة + س + ا + ر + د

The shapes (ة and ة) within words:

دَجاجة	وَردة	زَوْجة	سَيّارة
dajaaja	*warda*	*zawja*	*sayyaara*
(a chicken)	(a flower)	(wife)	(car)

When a word ending in *taa marbuuTa* (ة, ة) is followed by a suffix, such as a possessive pronoun, it becomes a regular *taa* (ت) in both writing and pronunciation. For example:

sayyaara + *ii* (my) = *sayyaaratii* (my car) سَيّارتي = ي + سَيّارة

When a word ending in *taa marbuuTa* is part of a possessive phrase, the *taa marbuuTa* is pronounced as a regular *taa* (ت), but its written form does not change. For Example:

سَيّارة+الأُستاذ = سَيّارة الأُستاذ

sayyaara + *al-ustaaz* = *sayyaaratu l-ustaaz* (The teacher's car)

The shapes ة and ة in various calligraphic styles:

Kufic	Diwani	Ta'liq	Ruq'a	Thuluth	Nasakh
	ة	ة	ة	ة	ة
	ـة	ـة	ـة	ـة	ـة

Shape Name: *laam alif*

The *laam alif* is not part of the
Arabic alphabet, but a shape that
combines two letters: *laam* (ل)

لام الف   *laam-alif*

and *alif* (ا). Because the *alif* is a non-connector, the shape
laam-alif (لا) does not connect to any letter that follows it.
This combination, pronounced *laa* means *no* in Arabic. When
the letter *laam* is preceded by *alif*, then it may be part of the
definite article *al..* (ال...), which will be discussed on page 72.

Examples	Location / Position / Connection	Shape / Form
الاول	Isolated / Independent / Initial Not connected to any letter	لا
ثلاثة	Medial / Final / End Connected to preceding letter	لا...

Printed form in standard script

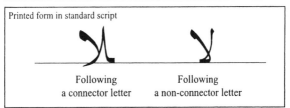

Following
a connector letter   Following
a non-connector letter

To write the shape, follow the arrows:

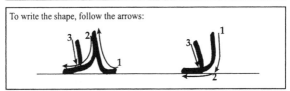

ا ب ت ث ج ح خ د ذ ر ز س ش ص ض ط ظ ع غ ف ق ك ل م ن هـ و ي

Connecting the shape لا :

H+l+aa+l = Halaal

'a+w+l+aa+d = 'awlaad

s+l+aa+m = salaam

d+l+aa+l = dalaal

Writing Direction ←

ح + ل + ا + ل = حلال

أ + و + ل + ا + د = أولاد

س + ل + ا + م = سَلام

د + ل + ا + ل = دَلال

The shape لا in combination with other letters (*alif* is long vowel **aa**):

حَلال
Halaal
(permissible)

سَلام
salaam
(peace)

أوْلاد
'awlaad
(children)

دَلال
dalaal
(*fem.* name)

The shape لا in combination with other letters (*alif* is a *hamza* seat **'a,'u,'i**):

الإبن
al-'ibn
(the son)

الأمير
al-'amiir
(the prince)

الأوّل
al-'awwal
(the first)

الأُخْت
al-'ukht
(the sister)

The shape لا in various calligraphic styles:

Diwani   *Ta'liq*   *Ruq'a*   *Thuluth*   *Nasakh*

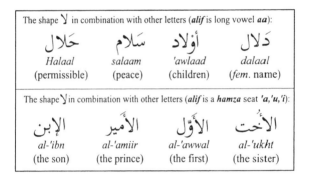

Variations of لا
in the *Kufic* style

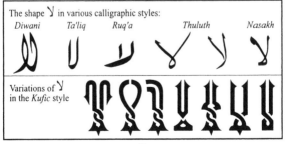

69

Variations of the *hamza*

تنوعات الهمزة (ؤ ئ)

hamza variations

As mentioned earlier, the *hamza* is a sign that is not part of the Arabic alphabet. The **alif** at the beginning of a word is always a seat for the *hamza* and it takes the sound of its vowel: (*a*, *u*, or *i*). When the *hamza* occurs in the middle or at the end of a word, the *yaa* ي and the *waaw* و serve as seats (*kursi* كرسي) for the *hamza*. When the *hamza* is followed or preceded by a *Damma* (ُ) or a long vowel *uu* (و), then the *hamza* is written on top of the *waaw* (ؤ). When the *hamza* is followed or preceded by a *kasra* (ِ) or a long vowel *ii* (ي), then the *hamza* is written on top of the *yaa* (ئ ئ ى). When the *yaa* serves as a seat for the *hamza*, it does not have any dots. The following charts show some examples of *hamza* variations.

Notes on *kursi waaw* (*hamza* with a *waaw* seat)	Example	Shape / Form
In the *kursi waaw*, the *waaw* is not connected to any letter. The *hamza* is preceded by a long vowel *uu*.	رؤوف *ra'uuf* (*masc.* name)	ؤ
In the *kursi waaw*, the *waaw* is connected to the preceding letter. The *hamza* is preceded by a *Damma*.	فُؤاد *fu'aad* (*masc.* name)	ؤ

The *hamza* with a *waaw* seat ؤ in various words:

رُؤوس	لُؤلؤ	بُؤس	سُؤال
ru'uus	*lu'lu'*	*bu's*	*su'aal*
(heads)	(pearl)	(misery)	(question)

ا ب ت ث ج ح خ د ذ ر ز س ش ص ض ط ظ ع غ ف ق ك ل م ن هـ و ي

Location / Position / Connection / Notes	Examples	Shape / Form
The *hamza* with a *yaa* seat (*kursi yaa*). The *yaa* is not connected to any letter, and the *hamza* is preceded by a *kasra*.	قارئ *qaari'* (reader)	ئ
The *hamza* with a *yaa* seat (*kursi yaa*). The *yaa* is connected to the following letter, and the *hamza* is followed by a *kasra*.	عائشة ^c*aa'isha* (*fem.* name)	ئ...
The *hamza* with a *yaa* seat (*kursi yaa*). The *yaa* is connected to both sides, and the *hamza* is followed by a *kasra*.	سُئِل *su'ila* (being asked)	...ئـ...
The *hamza* with a *yaa* seat (*kursi yaa*). The *yaa* is connected to the preceding letter, and the *hamza* is preceded by a *kasra*.	شاطئ *shaaTi'* (beach)	...ئ

Arabic words are generally derived or structured from a three consonant root (*jadhir* جذر). The *hamza* (ء) can be part of the root. Here are some examples of words derived from the root *s - ' - l* (س ء ل):

سُؤال
su'aal
(question)

أسئِلة
as'ila
(questions)

سَأَلَ
sa'ala
(he asked)

مسؤولية
mas'uuliya
(responsibility)

مسؤول
mas'uul
(responsible)

مسألة
mas'ala
(matter)

71

Arabic nouns are either definite or indefinite. There is no indefinite article in Arabic equivalent to the English **a** or **an**. Definite nouns are either proper nouns such as Egypt (*miSr* مصر), or begin with the definite article *al* (الـ), which is a prefix combining the letters *alif* (ا) and *laam* (ل). It is equivalent to the English *the*. Examples:

al-bayt (the house) البيت   *bayt* (house) بيت

In written Arabic, both letters are written (الـ), but in pronunciation, the letter that follows ل determines if *laam* is pronounced or assimilated. The Arabic letters are divided into two categories: moon letters (*qamariyya* قمرية) and sun letters (*shamsiyya* شمسية). With moon letters, the sound of ل is not affected, while sun letters are doubled with a *shadda* (ّ) and the ل is assimilated or silent.

Moon (*qamariyya*) letters: ا ب ج ح خ ع غ ف ق ك م هـ و ي		
بنت – البنت	باب – الباب	قمر – القمر
al-bint	*al-baab*	*al-qamar*
(the girl)	(the door)	(the moon)
ولد – الولد	جمل – الجمل	قهوة – القهوة
al-walad	*al-jamal*	*al-qahwa*
(the boy)	(the camel)	(the coffee)

Sun (*shamsiyya*) letters: ت ث د ذ ر ز س ش ص ض ط ظ ل ن		
سلام – السلام	شاي – الشاي	شمس – الشمس
as-salaam	*ash-shaay*	*ash-shams*
(the peace)	(the tea)	(the sun)
درس – الدرس	صحة – الصحة	نور – النور
ad-dars	*aS-SiHa*	*an-nuur*
(the lesson)	(the health)	(the light)

More on *alif & hamza*

alif madda (آ) الف مدة

When two *hamza* using the *alif* as a seat follow each other (أ + أ) or when a *hamza* is followed by a long vowel *alif* (١ + أ), then a *madda* symbol (آ) is used instead. It lengthens the pronunciation of the *alif*.

al-'aan (now) الآن *al-qur'aan* (the Qur'an) القرآن

Elidable *hamza - waSla* (ٱ) همزة الوصل

The *alif* in definite nouns that start with (الـ) is always a seat for the *hamza*. When these nouns are preceded by other words, the *hamza* is dropped in both writing and pronunciation and replaced by a symbol called **waSla** (وصلة), which means elidable or connecting *hamza*.

fii al-madrasa (in school) is pronounced *fil madrasa* في المدرسة

Dagger *alif* (ـٰ) الف مخفية

An old spelling dating back to the writing of the Qur'an القرآن has survived in a number of words and names. This old spelling omits the letter *alif*, but in completely vocalized text, the *alif* is represented by a small dagger or miniature *alif*. Notice the dagger *alif* in the following words:

لٰكن هٰذه هٰذا

laakin (but) *haadhihi* (this *f.*) *haadhaa* (this *m.*)

---

alif maqSuura (ى) الف مقصورة

The *alif maqSuura* is an *alif* in the shape of a *yaa* (ى). It is another spelling dating back to the writing of the Qur'an. It only occurs at the end of a word and is pronounced as a regular *alif (aa)*. Most names that end with the *alif maqSuura* are feminine names:

ليلى سلمى منى

laylaa (Layla) *salmaa* (Salma) *munaa* (Mona)

Basic Language Structure   Case Endings

In formal written, all nouns and adjectives have case endings. These vary according to the role of the word in the sentence. The *nominative* case is used for the sentence subject, and, in nominative sentences, for the predicate. The *accusative* case is used mainly with verb objects and adverbial expressions. The *genitive* case is used primarily with nouns that follow a preposition.

In completely vocalized texts, nouns with the definite article (*al-* الـ) are marked with different short vowels, depending on their case. Indefinite nouns can be marked with a symbol called *tanwiin*. The opening vowel of the *tanwiin* differs with each case.

	Case	Name	Sound	Symbol	Arabic
Definite Nouns	Nominative	*Damma*	u	ُ	ضمة
	Accusative	*fat-Ha*	a	َ	فتحة
	Genitive	*kasra*	i	ِ	كسرة
Indefinite Nouns	Nominative	*tanwiin aD-Damm*	un	ٌ	تنوين الضم
	Accusative	*tanwiin al-fatH*	an	ً	تنوين الفتح
	Genitive	*tanwiin al-kasr*	in	ٍ	تنوين الكسر

Note: The case endings of accusative indefinite nouns, *tanwiin al-fatH*, requires an *alif* seat ا .

74

Using the Arabic equivalent of the word *house*, **bayt** بيت, let's explore the variations for each case in both the definite and indefinite. Sample sentences are provided.

Nominative Definite:

bayt بيت ... ➜ *al-baytu* البيتُ

This house is beautiful. *haadaa l-baytu jamiilun* هذا البيتُ جميلٌ

Accusative Definite:

bayt بيت ... ➜ *al-bayta* البيتَ

I bought the house. *ishtaraytu l-bayta* اشتريتُ البيتَ

Genitive Definite:

bayt بيت ... ➜ *al-bayti* البيتِ

I live in the house. *askunu fii l-bayti* اسكُن في البيتِ

Nominative indefinite:

bayt بيت ... ➜ *baytun* بيتٌ

This is a beautiful house. *haadaa baytun jamiilun* هذا بيتٌ جميلٌ

Accusative indefinite:

bayt بيت ... ➜ *baytan* بيتاً

I bought a new house. *ishtaraytu baytan jadiidan* اشتريتُ بيتاً جديداً

Genitive indefinite:

bayt بيت ... ➜ *baytin* بيتٍ

I live in new house. *askunu fii baytin jadiidin* اسكُن في بيتٍ جديدٍ

75

All words in Arabic are either masculine (*mudhakkar* مذكر) or
feminine (*mu'anath* مؤنث). There is no common gender and no
word for *it*, so objects and animals are classified as مذكر or مؤنث.
In general, you can recognize feminine words by one of the following
features:

1. With a few exceptions, they end with a *taa marbuuTa* (ة ـة), e. g.

  شجرة   *shajara* (tree)   زوجة   *zawja* (wife)

2- Words that refer to a female, e. g.

  بنت   *bint* (daughter)   أخت   *ukht* (sister)

3- Parts of the body that occur in pairs, e. g.

  يد   *yadd* (hand)   عين   *ᶜayn* (eye)

There are also a number of feminine nouns that do not have those
features. These need to be learned individually. Examples:

  صحراء   *SaHraa'* (desert)   شمس   *shams* (sun)

In general, you can add the *taa marbuuTa* (ة ـة) to nouns and
adjectives to make them feminine. Adjectives normally follow nouns
and they have to agree with them in gender.

  استاذ طويل   *ustaadh Tawiil* (a tall teacher *m.*)

  استاذة طويلة   *ustaadha Tawiila* (a tall teacher *f.*)

  طالب صغير   *Taalib Saghiir* (a young student *m.*)

  طالبة صغيرة   *Taaliba Saghiira* (a young student *f.*)

The *taa marbuuTa* (ة ـة) can also be added to relative adjectives that
denote origin, affiliation, profession, or occupation.

مترجم – مترجمة	متخصص – متخصصة	مصري – مصرية
(translator)	(specialized)	(Egyptian)

Arabic has 3 kinds of pronouns: subject, possessive, and object.

object	possessive	subject
-nii (me) ني	-ii (my) ي	anaa (I) أنا
-ka /ak (you m.) لكَ	-ka /ak (your m.) لكَ	anta (you m.) أنتَ
-ki /ik (you f.) لكِ	-ki /ik (your f.) لكِ	anti (you f.) أنتِ
-hu (him) هُ	-hu (his) هُ	huwa (he) هُوَ
-haa (her) ها	-haa (her) ها	hiya (she) هِيَ
-naa (us) نا	-naa (our) نا	naHnu (we) نَحنُ
-kum (you pl.) كُم	-kum (your pl.) كُم	antum (you pl.) أنتُم
-hum (them) هُم	-hum (their) هُم	hum (they) هُم

Subject pronouns are detached or separate pronouns that are used in
basic sentences and to give emphasis:

> *ana ustaaz* (I am a teacher)   أنا أستاذ

> *huwa Taalib* (he is a student)   هو طالب

> *hiya jamiila* (she is beautiful)   هي جميلة

Possessive and object pronouns are suffixes that attach to a noun to
indicate possession, or to a verb to indicate the verb-object:

> *kitaabuha* (her book)   كتاب + هي (ها) = كتابها

> *baytuhu* (his house)   بيت + هو (ه) = بيته

> *yudarrisunii* (he teaches me)   يدرّس + انا = يدرّسني

> *yudarrisukum* (he teaches you pl.) يدرّس + انتم = يدرّسكم

A basic sentence in Arabic includes a subject called *mubtada'* (مبتدأ)
and a predicate called *khabar* (خبر). These sentences can exist
without verbs. The subject can be a noun or a pronoun. The predicate
can be another noun, an adjective, a sentence, or a phrase.

Examples:

خالد طالب

khaalid Taalib (Khalid is a student)

خالد لبناني

khaalid lubnaanii (Khalid is Lebanese)

خالد يدرس في جامعة بيروت

khaalid yadrus fii jaami^c at bayruut
(Khalid studies in the University of Beirut)

البيت كبير

al-baytu kbiir (The house is big)

هي استاذة في جامعة بيروت

hiyya ustaaza fii jaami^c at bayruut
(She is a teacher in the University of Beirut)

In general, the predicate (خبر) follows the subject (مبتدأ), but in
sentences that indicate possession, the subject will follow the
predicate. **For example:**

^c indii bayt jadiid (I have a new house) عندي بيت جديد

In this sentence, *bayt* (house) is the subject, and *^c indii* (at me, for me)
is the predicate. The preposition (*^c ind*) can be attached to pronouns to
express the concept of possession (to have).

One basic phrase in Arabic combines two nouns to form a possessive construction. This phrase is called *iDaafa* (الاضافة) and consists of two parts. The phrase is usually definite and expresses the possessive concept of *(the .... of ....)*. Only the second part takes the definite article. In *iDaafa* phrases, the *taa marbuuta* (ة) of the first part is always pronounced as ت. Only the second part can be attached to a possessive pronoun. Here are some examples:

بيت خالد

baytu khaalid (The house of Khalid)

سيارة الاستاذ

sayyaratu l-ustaaz (The teacher's car)

جامعة بيروت

jamiᶜat bayruut (The University of Beirut)

بنت خالي

bint khaalii (The daughter of my uncle or my cousin)

Adjectives must agree with the nouns they modify in case endings, gender, quantity, and whether the noun is definite or indefinite.

Plural	Dual (2)	Singular
(الـ)طالب (الـ)جيد	(الـ)طالبان (الـ)جيدان	(الـ)طلاب (الـ)جيدون
(الـ)طالبة (الـ)جيدة	(الـ)طالبتان (الـ)جيدتان	(الـ)طالبات (الـ)جيدات

The Dual ends with ان / ين , the masculine plural ends with ون/ ين, and the feminine plural ends with ات . One exception to this rule is the non-human plural, which is the same as feminine singular.

Arabic words are based on a trilateral (three-radical) root combined with a pattern called a *wazin* الوزن. A *wazin* consists of prefixes or suffixes, and one or more vowels. In Arabic grammar, the three radicals serve as the pattern for creating words from other roots. The chart below presents words derived from the root k-t-b (ك ت ب) root. They all relate to the concept of writing or books. The order follows the one found in Arabic-English dictionaries, which are organized according to the root of words.

Structure & Notes	Pattern	Word
Past tense verb (*he wrote*) For conjugation, see P. 82	فَعَلَ	كَتَبَ
Present tense verb (*he writes*) For conjugation, see P. 81	يَفْعُل	يَكْتُب
Gerund or verbal noun (*writing*)	فِعالة	كِتابة
Past tense verb (*he corresponded with someone*)	فاعَلَ	كاتَبَ
Past tense verb (*corresponded with each other*)	تَفاعَلَ	تَكاتَبَ
Noun (*book*)	فِعال	كِتاب
Noun (*office*)	مَفْعَل	مَكْتَب
Noun (*library*)	مَفْعَلة	مَكْتَبة
Noun/active participle (*writer, author*)	فاعِل	كاتِب
Noun/passive participle (something written, e.g. *a letter*)	مَفْعول	مَكْتوب

Arabic verbs have only two tenses: perfect (past tense, completed actions called *maaDii* ماضي), and imperfect (present tense, incomplete, called *muDaariᶜ* مضارع). There is no infinitive of the Arabic verb, only a trilateral root based on three consonants or radicals. Arabic verbs consist of a stem and a subject marker (the action doer), in the form of a prefix or a suffix as shown in the charts below. Verbs with a prefix mostly indicate the present or future tense, while verbs with a suffix indicate the past tense. The pattern of the three radicals ف ع ل is used as a model for the structure of Arabic verbs.

Present Tense of (to study) - stem d-r-s (س ر د)				
	Model	**Example**	**Pattern**	**Pron.**
anaa (I)	أ....	أدرُس	أفعُل	انا
anta (you m.)	ت....	تدرُس	تَفعُل	انتَ
anti (you f.)	ت.....ين/ت.....ي	تدرسين / تدرُسي	تَفعُلين / تَفعُلي	انتِ
huwa (he)	ي....	يدرُس	يَفعُل	هو
hiya (she)	ت....	تدرُس	تَفعُل	هي
naHnu (we)	ن....	ندرُس	نَفعُل	نحن
antum (you pl.)	ت.....ون/ت.....وا	تدرُسون / تدرُسوا	تَفعُلون / تَفعُلوا	انتم
hum (they)	ي.....ون/ي.....وا	يدرُسون / يدرُسوا	يَفعُلون / يَفعُلوا	هم

Notes:

1- Prefixes and suffixes are added to the stem of the verb, which usually consists of three consonants. This applies to all present tense verbs.

2- The first consonant of the stem has no vowel. The third consonant normally carries a *Damma*, while the second consonant may have a *fatHa*, *Damma*, or *kasra*.

3- For *anti*, *antum*, and *hum* two forms exist depending on the grammatical context. The default form is the one that ends with ن .

Past tense verbs or completed actions (*maaDii* ماضي) use suffixes to indicate the subject. The present and past tenses use the same stem. The masculine singular conjugation (the *he* form) is used as a model for conjugating other verbs. It is also called the dictionary form since it has no suffixes or prefixes.

Past Tense of (study) - stem/ root *d-r-s* (د ر س)				
	Model	**Example**	**Pattern**	**Pron.**
anaa (I)	....تُ	دَرَستُ	فَعَلتُ	انا
anta (you *m.*)	....تَ	دَرَستَ	فَعَلتَ	انتَ
anti (you *f.*)	....تِ	دَرَستِ	فَعَلتِ	انتِ
huwa (he)	......	دَرَسَ	فَعَلَ	هو
hiya (she)	....تْ	دَرَسَتْ	فَعَلَتْ	هي
naHnu (we)	....نا	دَرَسنا	فَعَلنا	نحن
antum (you *pl.*)	....تُم	دَرَستُم	فَعَلتُم	انتم
hum (they)	....وا	دَرَسوا	فَعَلوا	هـم

Sentences with perfect and imperfect tense verbs:

Sara **studies** at the University of Cairo سارة تَدرُس في جامعة القاهرة

We **study** the Arabic language نحن نَدرُس اللغة العربية

The students **study** Arabic literature الطلاب يدرُسون الادب العربي

Khalid **studied** in Beirut خالد دَرَسَ في بيروت

Sara **studied** at the university سارة دَرَسَتْ في الجامعة

My friends **studied** the Arabic language. اصدقائي دَرَسوا اللغة العربية

The imperative tense (*al-amr* الأمر) is used to give commands and orders. Its form depends on the person or group being addressed. Imperative verbs have a *hamza* with an *alif* seat as a prefix and carry either a *Damma* ـُ or a *kasra* ـِ vowel, depending on the vowel of the second radical of the stem in the present tense. This pattern mostly applies to basic and standard verbs of three radicals. The imperative of derived verbs follows different patterns. The chart below demonstrates conjugations in the imperative.

yadrus يدرُس (to study) - d,r,s (د ر س) stem				
	Model	**Example**	**Pattern**	**Pron.**
anta (you *m.*)	أ....ـ	أُدرُس	أُفعُل	انتَ
anti (you *f.*)	أ....ي	أُدرُسي	أُفعُلي	انتِ
antum (you *pl.*)	أ....وا	أُدرُسوا	أُفعُلوا	انتم

yajlis يجلِس (to sit) - j,l,s (ج ل س) stem				
anta (you *m.*)	إ....	إجلِس	إفعِل	انتَ
anti (you *f.*)	إ....ي	إجلِسي	إفعِلي	انتِ
antum (you *pl.*)	إ....وا	إجلِسوا	إفعِلوا	انتم

Notes:

1- The verb *yadrus* in the present tense has a *Damma* on the second radical of the stem of the verb (يدرُس), so the *hamza* prefix in the imperative takes a *Damma*, *udrus* أُدرُس .

2- The verb *yajlis* in the present tense has a *kasra* on the second radical of the stem (يجلِس), so the *hamza* prefix in the imperative takes a *kasra*, *ijlis* إجلِس .

The future tense (المستقبل) in Arabic is expressed by adding suffixes to the present tense form. The word *sawfa* سوف, or its shorter form, the letter *siin* ـس , are used to express the future in the manner of the English *will* and *shall*.

Examples of the future tense:

سوف أذهب الى مصر السنة القادمة

sawfa adh-hab ilaa miSr as-sana al-qaadima
I will go to Egypt next year.

سندرس اللغة العربية في المستقبل

sanadrus al-lugha l-ᶜarabiyya fi l-mustaqbal
We will study Arabic in the future.

A common expression in Arabic is *in shaa' allah* ان شاء الله , which means "God willing." It is used by most Arabs when talking about future events.

Derived Forms of the Basic Verb:

Most Arabic verbs have a basic form consisting of the pattern (فَعَلَ). Letters can be added to this form to give the verb a different but usually related meaning. Western linguists have assigned these forms the Roman numeral I-X. They are used by Arabic-English dictionaries and need to be memorized. The following chart gives the forms with their patterns and the patterns' meanings. Examples of common verbs are provided for each of the forms.

Form	Pattern	Pattern Meaning	Sample Verbs (Past Tense)	الوزن
I	faʿala	The basic or simple meaning of the verb. All other forms are derived from this one. It is also known as a "stripped verb." Each derived or increased form has one or more additional letters giving it a new meaning that has some association with the stripped verb.	عَرَفَ to get to know	فَعَلَ
	faʿila		كَتَبَ to write	فَعِلَ
	faʿula		كَسَرَ to break	فَعُلَ
			عَلِمَ to know	
			قَطَعَ to cut	
II	faʿʿala	Indicates the strengthening, or intensifying, of the verb meaning. Represents the causing or performing of an action on someone or something. Transitive (the verb takes an object).	عَرَّفَ to introduce	فَعَّلَ
			كَتَّبَ to make someone write	
			كَسَّرَ to break into pieces	
			عَلَّمَ to teach	
			قَطَّعَ to cut into pieces	
III	faaʿala	Indicates the relating of the action to or attempting the action on another person. Reciprocal.	كَاتَبَ to correspond with	فَاعَلَ
			قَاطَعَ to cut off, interrupt	
IV	afʿala	Makes intransitive verbs transitive. Also indicates causation in transitive verbs.	أعْلَمَ to inform	أفْعَلَ
			أقْطَعَ to divide up (land)	
V	tafaʿʿala	Converts Form II (and occasionally I) to the reflexive mode. The verbs, derived from nouns connoting prestige or quality, identify the subject with the source nouns.	تَعَرَّفَ to become acquainted	تَفَعَّلَ
			تَكَسَّرَ to be broken in pieces	
			تَعَلَّمَ to learn	
			تَقَطَّعَ to be chopped up	
VI	tafaaʿala	Converts Form III to the reflexive. Implies action mutual between subject and object.	تَعَارَفَ to become acquainted with one another	تَفَاعَلَ
			تَكَاتَبَ to write to each other	
			تَقَاطَعَ to intersect	
VII	infaʿala	Converts the verb to the passive voice.	انْكَسَرَ to get broken	انْفَعَلَ
			انْقَطَعَ to be cut off	
VIII	iftaʿala	Converts Form I to the reflexive. Used to twist the meaning of the base verb.	اعْتَرَفَ to confess, admit	افْتَعَلَ
			اقْتَطَعَ to cut off a part	
IX	ifʿalla	Indicates the gaining and maintenance of attributes.	احْمَرَّ to become red	افْعَلَّ
X	istafʿala	Indicates the action with the verb object.	اسْتَقْطَعَ to deduct	اسْتَفْعَلَ
			اسْتَعْلَمَ to inquire	

The gerund, or verbal noun, is called *maSdar* (المصدر). It expresses the verb's action. (The gerund of the English *to read* is *reading*.) The gerunds of most verbs follow standard patterns. The only exceptions are simple (Form I) verbs. It is best to learn these verbs and their gerunds simultaneously. Most dictionaries are helpful in this and present the gerund after the verb in their entries.

The chart below summarizes the gerund of the derived verb forms with examples and their patterns. The **Gerund** column presents the gerund patterns underlined, and the gerund of the verbs from the **Example** column.

Form	Pattern	Example	Gerund
I	فَعَل	كتَبَ to write	*Varies*
	فَعِل	قطَعَ to cut	
	فَعُل	درَسَ to study	
II	فعَّل	درَّسَ to teach	التفعيل التدريس
III	فاعَل	قاطَعَ to boycott	المُفاعلة المُقاطعة
IV	أفعَل	أقطَعَ to divide up (land)	الافعال الاقطاع
V	تفعَّل	تعلَّمَ to learn	التفعُّل التعلُّم
VI	تفاعَل	تقاطَعَ to intersect	التفاعُل التقاطُع
VII	إنفعَل	إنقطَعَ to be chopped off	الانفعال الانقطاع
VIII	إفتعَل	إعترَفَ to confess, admit	الافتعال الاعتراف
IX	إفعَلّ	إحمَرَّ to become red	الافعلال الاحمرار
X	إستفعَل	إستأجَرَ to rent	الاستفعال الاستئجار

Question Word	Sample Sentence	السؤال
hal? a yes/no question (is/are/were, etc.)	هل احمد في البيت؟ Is Ahmad at home?	هَل
maa? What? (asking about things)	ما هذا؟ What (is) this (*m.*)?	ما
maadhaa? What? (+ a verb)	ماذا يدرس أحمد؟ What (is) Ahmad studying?	ماذا
man? Who?	مَن هو الاستاذ الجديد؟ Who (is) the new teacher?	مَن
ayna? Where?	أين تسكن؟ Where (do) you live?	أينَ
kayfa? How?	كيف حالك؟ How (are) you?	كَيفَ
kam? How many?	كم سنة درستَ العربية؟ How many years have you studied Arabic?	كَم
mataa? When?	متى تسافر الى الاردن؟ When (are) you traveling to Jordan?	مَتى
ayy? Which (*m.*)?	أي كتاب تُحب؟ Which book (do) you like?	أيّ
ayyat? Which (*f.*)?	أية مدينة تُحب؟ Which city (do) you like?	أيّة

Some of the interrogative particles above can be combined with prepositions, as in these examples:

عن ماذا؟	في أي؟	من أين؟
About what?	In which?	From where?

Arabic Numerals

Arabic numerals (الاعداد العربية *al-'a^{c}daad al-^{c}arabiya*) are written in two forms: standard and Hindi. **(The standard form appears in the written column in the chart below)**. The *Hindi* numbers, which are primarily used in the eastern Arab countries, are written from left to right.

Example:

$$1563 = \text{١٥٦٣} \qquad 146 = \text{١٤٦} \qquad 67 = \text{٦٧}$$

In formal written Arabic, more than one form exists for each number based on grammatical context and the gender of the object(s) being counted. The spoken/colloquial form of the numbers is also used in telling time. The only exceptions are 1:00 (*waHida*) and 2:00 (*thintayn*).

Arabic	Spoken	Written	Hindi
0	*Sifr*	صفر	٠
1	*waaHid*	واحد	١
2	*ithnaan/ ithnayn*	اثنان\ اثنين	٢
3	*thalaatha*	ثلاثة	٣
4	*arba^{c}a*	اربعة	٤
5	*khamsa*	خمسة	٥
6	*sitta*	ستة	٦
7	*sab^{c}a*	سبعة	٧
8	*thamaanya*	ثمانية	٨
9	*tis^{c}a*	تسعة	٩
10	*^{c}ashara*	عشرة	١٠

11	*iHda ᶜsh*	احدى عشر	١١
12	*itna ᶜsh*	اثنى عشر	١٢
13	*thalaTa ᶜsh*	ثلاثة عشر	١٣
14	*arbaᶜTa ᶜsh*	اربعة عشر	١٤
15	*khamsTa ᶜsh*	خمسة عشر	١٥
16	*sit Ta ᶜsh*	ستة عشر	١٦
17	*sabᶜTa ᶜsh*	سبعة عشر	١٧
18	*thaman Ta ᶜsh*	ثمانية عشر	١٨
19	*tisᶜTa ᶜsh*	تسعة عشر	١٩
20	*ᶜishriin*	عشرون اعشرين	٢٠
21	*waaHid wa ᶜishriin*	واحد وعشرين	٢١
22	*ithneen wa ᶜishriin*	اثنين وعشرين	٢٢
23	*thalata wa ᶜishriin*	ثلاثة وعشرين	٢٣
30	*thalaathiin*	ثلاثون ا ثلائين	٣٠
40	*arbᶜiin*	اربعون ا اربعين	٤٠
50	*khamsiin*	خمسون\ خمسين	٥٠
60	*sittiin*	ستون \ ستين	٦٠
70	*sabᶜiin*	سبعون \سبعين	٧٠
80	*thamaniin*	ثمانون \ ثمانين	٨٠
90	*tisᶜiin*	تسعون \ تسعين	٩٠

100	*miyya*	مئة \ مائة	۱۰۰
106	*miyya w sitta*	مئة وستة	۱۰٦
125	*miyya w khamsa* *w ʿishriin*	مئة وخمسة وعشرون	۱۲٥
200	*miteen*	مئتان \ مئتين	۲۰۰
300	*thalath miyya*	ثلاث مائة	۳۰۰
537	*khams miyya* *w sabʿa w thalathiin*	خمس مائة وسبعة وثلاثون	٥۳۷
1000	*alf*	الف	۱۰۰۰
1000	*alfeen*	الفان \ الفين	۲۰۰۰
3000	*thalaathat aalaaf*	ثلاثة الاف	۳۰۰۰

Ordinal Numbers:

The ordinal numbers in Arabic are very similar to the cardinal numbers, except for *first* and *sixth*. The number's gender is changed from masculine to feminine by adding the *taa marbuuTa* (ة). The chart on the right shows the cardinal and ordinal numbers. In formal written Arabic, the definite feminine ordinal numbers are used to tell time except for 1:00. Examples:

first	أولى	أول	۱
second	ثانية	ثاني	۲
third	ثالثة	ثالث	۳
fourth	رابعة	رابع	٤
fifth	خامسة	خامس	٥
sixth	سادسة	سادس	٦
seventh	سابعة	سابع	۷
eighth	ثامنة	ثامن	۸
ninth	تاسعة	تاسع	۹
tenth	عاشرة	عاشر	۱۰

1:00   الساعة الواحدة

3:00   الساعة الثالثة

7:00   الساعة السابعة

Arabic Calligraphy (الخط العربي) is an Arabic and Islamic artform. It links the literary heritage of the Arabic language with the religion of Islam الاسلام. It is an artistic tradition of extraordinary beauty, richness and power. The Qur'an القرآن (the Muslim Holy Book) played a major role in the development and evolution of Arabic script and calligraphy. Calligraphy means "beautiful handwriting," and in Arabic it also means the "art of the pen" (فن القلم) and "the geometry of the spirit" (الهندسة الروحانية).

The first revelation of the Qur'an inspired Arab and Muslim artists to use calligraphy as an expression of spiritual and artistic identity. Arabic calligraphy has been used for centuries to decorate manuscripts, architectural buildings, and objects of daily life. Despite the diversity of the Arabic and Islamic world, Arabic calligraphy is a major unifying element of Islamic art. In addition to its spiritual value, calligraphy and inscriptions on architectural monuments serve as historical documents. It is an artform that utilizes every imaginable media including paper, wood, metal, glass, stone, ivory, and leather. Arabic calligraphy is also considered a form of worship and plays a major role in Arabic and Islamic cultures.

There are over 100 styles of Arabic calligraphy, but only six scripts (Kufic, Thuluth, Nasakh, Diwani, Ta'liq, and Riq'a) are considered major. These are shown on the next page. Zoomorphic calligraphy, in which words are shaped into human figures, birds, animals, and objects, was developed as a form of prayer.

The Art of Arabic Calligraphy جملة من نقل العربي

Kufic - named after the city of *Kufa* in Iraq. It is the oldest style.	الخط الكوفي
Thuluth - (*lit.* one third) is an ornamental style.	خط الثلث
Nasakh - (*lit.* copy) was used to copy the Qur'an.	خط النسخ
Ta'liq - (*lit.* hanging) is also called *Farsi* (Persian).	خط التعليق
Diwani - (*lit.* Royal Court) was the favorite script of Ottoman chancellery.	الخط الديواني
Riq'a - (*lit.* small sheet) is a simple style used in every day handwriting.	خط الرقعة
Zoomorphic - *is a style in which words take the shape of a human figure, a bird, an animal, or an object. This bird contains the phrase "In the name of God, the Merciful, the Compassionate."*	

Geometric Proportioning of Arabic Script:
The elements of proportion of Arabic script are: **1-** The height of the *alif* (|), which is a straight and vertical stroke (3-12) dots. **2-** The width of the *alif*, (the dot) which is the square impression formed by pressing the tip of the pen to the paper. **3-** An imaginary circle with *alif* as its diameter, within which all Arabic letters could be written.

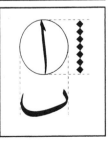

92